MARK to MARKET

Managing the Bank Portfolio Under FASB #115

John E. Bowen

A BANKLINE PUBLICATION
PROBUS PUBLISHING COMPANY
Chicago, Illinois
Cambridge, England

BANKLINE™

© 1994, Probus Publishing Company

ALL RIGHTS RESERVED. No part of this publication may be reproduced, stored in a retrieval system, or transmitted, in any form or by any means, electronic, mechanical, photocopying, recording, or otherwise, without the prior written permission of the publisher and the author.

This publication is designed to provide accurate and authoritative information in regard to the subject matter covered. It is sold with the understanding that the author and the publisher are not engaged in rendering legal, accounting, or other professional service.

Authorization to photocopy items for internal or personal use, or the internal or personal use of specific clients, is granted by PROBUS PUBLISHING COMPANY, provided that the U.S. $7.00 per page fee is paid directly to Copyright Clearance Center, 222 Rosewood Drive, Danvers, MA 01923, USA; Phone: 1-508-750-8400. For those organizations that have been granted a photocopy license by CCC, a separate system of payment has been arranged. The fee code for users of the Transactional Reporting Service is 1-55738-701-X/94/$00.00 + $7.00.

ISBN 1-55738-701X

Printed in the United States of America

IPC

2 3 4 5 6 7 8 9 0

CB/BJS

Probus books are available at quantity discounts when purchased for business, educational, or sales promotional use. For more information, please call the Director, Corporate / Institutional Sales at (800) 998-4644, or write:

Director, Corporate / Institutional Sales
Probus Publishing Company
1925 N. Clybourn Avenue
Chicago, IL 60614
PHONE (800) 998-4644   FAX (312) 868-6250

To my loving wife,
Debbie,
and children,
Ryan, John, Megan, and *Elizabeth.*

Table of Contents

Preface ... ix

1 A New Era in Investment Portfolio Management ... 1

    Classification of Investment Securities
    Impact on Investment Portfolio Management
    Impact on Financial Management
    Trends for the Future
    Summary

2 Liquidity and Capital at Risk ... 9

    Develop an Investment Plan
    Assess Interest Rate Risk and Liquidity Needs
    Determine Capital at Risk
    Impact on Financial Statement Ratios
    Summary

3 Classification of Investment Securities ... 25

    Investment Philosophy—Buy-and-Hold or Total Return?
    Strategies for Classifying Investment Securities
    How Much Is too Much?
    Mark-to-Market Worksheets
    Mark-to-Market Worksheet Classification Notes
    Investment Classification Recommendations
    Gains Trading and Other Financial Management Issues
    Summary

4 Managing the Investment Portfolio ... 49

    Is There Life after Mark-to-Market?
    Buy-and-Hold Investment Management
    Total Return Investment Management
    Total Return versus Buy-and-Hold
    Interest Rates
    Asset/Liability Management
    Mutual Funds
    Structured Debt Securities

Summary
Types of Structured Debt Securities

5 *Hedging the Portfolio with Derivatives*   65

Regulatory Concerns about Derivatives
Convexity
Interest Rate Swaps
Forwards
Forward Rate Agreement
Interest Rate Caps
Interest Rate Floors
Interest Rate Collars
Futures Contracts
Options
Interest Rate Volatility and the Investment Portfolio
Hedging the Investment Portfolio
Derivative Analytics and Operating Systems
Summary
Suggestions for Further Reading

6 *Accounting and Financial Reporting*   89

Mark-to-Market Accounting Summary
Investment Portfolio Accounting—A History of Changes
Investment Accounting System
General Ledger Accounting
Regulatory Reporting
Income Tax Considerations
Conclusion

7 *Investment Management Policy and Documentation*   107

Investment Policy
Illustrative Investment Policy
Authorized Investments
Classification of Investment Securities
Transfer between Categories of Investment
Unsuitable Investment Practices
Selection of Security Dealers
Duties and Responsibilities
Investment Trade Documentation

8 Conclusion and Future of Mark-to-Market   **119**
    Executive Summary
    The Futute of Mark-to-Market

Appendix A: Excerpts from An Examiner's Guide to Investments Products and Practices   **123**

Appendix B: Excerpts from FASB Statement No. 115   **141**

Preface

Several years ago I told Jim McNeil at Probus Publishing that I would like to write a book on managing the investment portfolio if mark-to-market accounting became a reality. I thought that this book was important because managing the portfolio in the 1990s was becoming increasingly complex, with a plethora of new investment products, the lowest interest rates in 20 to 30 years and emerging regulatory issues (e.g., risk based capital, interest rate risk proposal, FDICIA, etc.), not to mention recent banking issues such as weak loan demand and deposit outflows. After mark-to-market was scuttled by the American Institute of Certified Public Accountants (AICPA) and lost support at the Financial Accounting Standards Board (FASB), I had mixed emotions. However, investment mark-to-market was revived at the eleventh hour and I commenced writing this book.

Mark-to-Market: Managing the Portfolio Under FASB #115 is designed to help institutions make the strategic decisions required to implement market value accounting with the goal of having an investment portfolio that is high-yielding, marketable, and postured opportunistically against a wider variety of interest rate scenarios. Institutions should not underestimate the difficulty of managing the portfolio under Statement 115. The investment manager must purchase the right bond, for the right purpose, at the right time, for the right price, and now, place it in the right category. Decisions made now with respect to managing the portfolio will have a long term impact on investment income, liquidity and control of interest rate risk. Institutions must guard against unnecessarily restricting future investment activities and interest rate risk. Statement 115 provides institutions with a timely opportunity to upgrade the investment management function. Institutions that are ill-prepared to implement Statement 115 will have a more difficult time defending their plans for managing the portfolio.

Many of the concepts included in this book were developed by Wachovia for presentation at our Mark-to-Market Investment Conferences in August 1993. These conferences were attended by over 250 bankers who came with questions and comments that provided a forum to help fine-tune and validate principles on managing the portfolio under Statement 115. Speakers who helped make our conference a success included Wachovians Rick

Alspaugh, Steve Ashworth, Al DeForest, Bob Mayers, Ken McAllister, Bob McCoy, Dick Roberts, Jim Smith, and Mike Tierney, as well as Dick Brezovec and Dayton Lierley from Ernst & Young and Sharon Haas from Thompson BankWatch. I am indebted to these individuals—their efforts have made this book come to life with meaningful illustrations and examples. Other Wachovians that assisted with this project included Diane Dimmick, Earl Hartenstine, Verda Hennis, John Jackson, Alan Johnson, Hubbard Morris, George Paynter, Steve Slade, Phil Swentzel and Stuart Winikoff. In addition, I want to thank Owen Carney (Comptroller of the Currency), Jeanne Krips (KeyCorp), Bill Lovern (Nomura) and Bob Wilkins (FASB) for their counsel and insights on mark-to-market and other topics over the years. Finally, I want to express my sincere appreciation to Andy Beard, Mike Martin, and Bob Mayers from the Wachovia Bond and Money Market Group for allowing me to complete this important work.

Of course, this book would not have been possible without the patience and support of my wife, Debbie, during those uncountable hours of writing which disrupted our family life.

Chapter 1:
A New Era in Investment Portfolio Management

Table of Contents—

Classification of Investment Securities
Impact on Investment Portfolio Management
  Implementation Planning
  Change in Investment Philosophy
Impact on Financial Management
  Return of Asset/Liability Management
  Managing Capital
Trends for the Future
Summary

On May 31, 1993, the Financial Accounting Standards Board (FASB) issued Statement No. 115, "Accounting for Certain Investments in Debt and Equity Securities" (Statement 115). The advent of Statement 115 marks the beginning of a new era in investment portfolio management.

Statement 115 will have a far-reaching effect on the management of the investment portfolio, requiring banks to classify individual securities into one of the following categories:

Held-to-Maturity—Debt securities that the institution has the positive intent and ability to hold to maturity; reported at amortized cost.

Trading securities—Debt and equity securities purchased to generate earnings through short-term gains; reported at market value with gains/losses recorded in earnings.

Available-for-Sale—Debt and equity securities not classified as held-to-maturity or trading; reported at market value with gains/losses recorded (net of tax effect) as a separate component of equity.

This book is designed to help institutions make the strategic decisions required to implement market-value accounting with the goal of having an investment portfolio that is high yielding, marketable, and postured opportunistically against a wider variety of interest rate scenarios.

CLASSIFICATION OF INVESTMENT SECURITIES

The "held-to-maturity" test is more stringent than in the past. At acquisition, an institution must establish the positive intent to hold the security to maturity, rather than just have the lack of intent to sell the security as in the past. If there is even a remote possibility that a security might be sold, it is not appropriate to carry that security at amortized cost.

When management has the positive intent to hold a security to maturity, it must decide to disregard the effects of changes in factors such as market interest rates, prepayment risk, or foreign exchange rates.

The initial classification of investments, discussed in Chapter 2, is probably the most difficult aspect of implementing Statement 115. Each institution is different, and there is no right or wrong way to classify investments into held-to-maturity or available-for-sale categories. There is no minimum or maximum level of securities that should be allocated to either account classification.

Because of the impact of available-for-sale investments on capital and liquidity, classifying investments requires an institution to perform a comprehensive assessment of interest rate risk and liquidity needs, as well as long-range capital planning for the contingency of an adverse bond market. Classification of investment securities should be evaluated in light of both *current and future* asset/liability management positions, as well as liquidity and capital planning needs. Developing a comprehensive plan for classifying investments, with consistent application, is essential to obtaining the approval of bank examiners and independent accountants for investment portfolio activities.

Individual securities targeted for the available-for-sale account should be analyzed based on the *total rate-of-return* performance. (See Chapter 4 for further discussion of total rate of return). This performance analysis may affect an institution's intent, ability or desire to hold a particular security in either available-for-sale or held-to-maturity categories.

Fixed-income investors, such as mutual funds, pension funds, and insurance companies, follow more of a total-return investment management style. Total-return investors actively manage their investments to take advantage of *expected* changes in interest rates and prepayments. The ability to sell investments without regard to original cost increases the opportunity to improve returns. However, even after adopting Statement 115, institutions cannot completely disregard the accounting cost basis because of related income statement and capital planning considerations involved in the sale of securities.

IMPACT ON INVESTMENT PORTFOLIO MANAGEMENT

The investment portfolio manager has had a tough job in the past—and it's about to get a lot tougher. Financial institutions must now make strategic decisions regarding the initial classification of the investment portfolio and develop ongoing business management policies guiding the use of securities to help manage interest rate risk and earnings and capital volatility. Decisions made now with respect to managing the portfolio will have a long-term impact on investment income, liquidity, and control of interest rate risk.

Implementation Planning

In addition to the initial classification of investments securities, there are numerous other issues, which must be addressed to successfully implement Statement 115, including the following:

- Educate upper management and the Board of Directors;
- Review implementation plan with independent accountants to get their thoughts and ideas on classifying securities, etc;
- Re-evaluate investment management philosophy for held-to-maturity, available-for-sale, and trading categories;
- Update investment policies and procedures;
- Review adequacy of investment accounting system, including timeliness and accuracy of bond pricing;
- Review financial, regulatory, tax, and management reporting; and
- Determine implementation timing—1993 or 1994.

Institutions should not underestimate the difficulty of managing the investment portfolio under Statement 115. Some institutions will mistakenly execute securities sales that jeopardize the classification of held-to-maturity and available-for-sale portfolios. Unfortunately, with Statement 115, you cannot rewrite history, and institutions may be required for mark-to-market investments intended to be held-to-maturity.

Change in Investment Philosophy

Institutions must guard against "winning the battle, but losing the war." That is, an institution may do a great job of limiting earnings and capital volatility in implementing Statement 115, but unnecessarily restrict future investment activities and interest rate risk. Or worse, take on *more* organizational interest rate risk because of an ill-advised change in investment strategies.

For most institutions, the timing of adopting Statement 115 could not be better. With the lowest interest rates in over 20 years, institutions have significant profits in their investment portfolios and adopting Statement 115 should result in an increase to capital. However, the legacy of Statement 115 will be how institutions manage the investment portfolio in an adverse market. Portfolio managers should hope for the best but plan for the worst. The game plan your institution follows for Statement 115 must stand the test of time during different markets.

Investment management has always been more of an art than a science. Portfolio managers must overcome a built-in handicap. When economic activity is strong and rates are high, funds available for investments are limited because loan demand is strong. The result: Financial institutions make more loans and fewer investments. When loan demand is weak and rates are low, funds available for investments are plentiful. The result: Financial institutions make more investments and fewer loans. As a result of these cycles, financial institutions tend to invest more when rates are low and less when rates are high. The prolonged bull market of the late 1980s and early 1990s has allowed institutions to overcome this built-in handicap.

The current sharply sloped yield curve is both a blessing and a curse. It provides investors with more downside risk than upside potential. It has widened interest spreads but also is causing an outflow of consumer savings to higher-return investments. This could eventually lead to funding shortfalls and higher deposit costs. A rise in short-term rates would narrow interest margins and put downward pressure on investment portfolio market values.

IMPACT ON FINANCIAL MANAGEMENT

Statement 115 has already affected the financial management of banking. Since 1990, when the FASB began its review of mark-to-market accounting for investment securities, institutions have been planning for the issuance of Statement 115.

Statement 115 prevents securities in the held-to-maturity account from being sold for purposes of managing the institution's interest rate risk posture. This may limit an institution's flexibility to respond to economic opportunities and change. Additionally, sales or transfers from the held-to-maturity account may cause scrutiny of other investments in the held-to-maturity category. These restrictions make it desirable for interest rate risk and liquidity to be managed using a total balance sheet perspective and not just an asset-directed strategy, which some institutions have used in the past. Statement 115 may lead some institutions to make greater use of off-balance sheet products such as swaps, options, and futures to manage interest rate risk. It may lead other institutions to reduce the size of investment portfolios and increase loans, which are not marked-to-market.

Return of Asset/Liability Management

The principles of Statement 115 make it important for an institution to accurately measure interest rate risk and adopt a risk management policy that will enhance flexibility and maintain earnings stability in a variety of rate environments. The interest rate risk posture of the institution should be evaluated on a regular basis to assure that a coordinated and consistent investment management philosophy is implemented. Liquidity needs should also be forecasted and investment strategies adjusted to accommodate the institution's anticipated funding needs.

Institutions that have up-to-date asset/liability management models will be better able to obtain the interest rate risk information required to manage the investment portfolio under Statement 115. This is an opportune time to assess the resource requirements of the asset/liability management and investment functions, as well as the investment accounting system.

Managing Capital

Statement 115 has created a conflict between managing interest rate risk and managing capital. This conflict will make it more difficult to manage the investment portfolio, particularly under adverse market conditions. Compounding this conflict is the 1992 passage of FDICIA which imposes severe penalties for institutions with capital shortfalls. In adopting Statement 115 it is uncertain how regulators will handle write-ups and write-downs of capital for Tier I and Tier II capital purposes.

For institutions with just five to 10 percent of total assets in an available-for-sale investment category, the reduction of capital during an upward rate cycle can be quite significant. To mitigate capital volatility, one strategy for adopting Statement 115 is to shorten the duration of the available-for-sale investments. Banks should periodically calculate the potential capital impact of holding available-for-sale investments. One method for calculating this capital sensitivity is illustrated in Chapter 2. Similarly, rather than endure market risk in the available-for-sale portfolio, or invest at current rate levels in the held-to-maturity portfolio, institutions may choose simply to reduce the size of the total investment portfolio, thereby conserving capital for underwriting loans rather than making investments.

With the current level of interest rates, most institutions will have an increase to capital upon adopting Statement 115. As indicated above, this capital could be short-lived depending on the strength or weakness of the bond market. Indeed, a capital surplus can turn into a capital shortfall in a matter of months. The irony is that institutions that are thinly capitalized should prudently maintain an available-for-sale portfolio with short duration—and lower yields—to protect capital. In general, institutions may wish to keep a capital cushion to absorb the volatility of mark-to-market investment accounting.

TRENDS FOR THE FUTURE

Without the explosive growth in the market for fixed-income securities, Statement 115 probably would not have been issued. Prior to 1985, institutions had three basic choices when purchasing investment securities: U.S. Governments, tax-frees, and corporates. Now, those three investment staples account for less than 50 percent of total investment securities.

Institutions now purchase from a wide array of investment products that did not exist ten years ago. Investment products are limited only by the imagination of Wall Street investment firms. Mortgage securities cover about every letter of the alphabet including: CMO tranches (e.g., PACs, TACs, VADMs, IOs, POs, Zs); ARMs (e.g., COFI, CMT, LIBOR); and passthroughs (e.g., GNMAs, FNMAs, and FHLMCs, GNOMES, DWARFS, and MIDGETS). A whole new language and technology have been developed to sell these securities with their own unique terminology: PSA, CPR, SMM, WAC, WAM, WAL, and FFIEC tests. In addition to mortgage securities, asset-backed securities (e.g., credit cards, automobile loans), and derivative securities, such as indexed amortizing swaps, allow institutions to manage risk positions in ways not dreamed of ten years ago. Even U.S. government agency securities are more complicated than ever before with "callables," "step-ups," and "dual-index, noncallable, consolidated" bonds dominating recent issues.

The dynamics of the investment market described above will continue to challenge portfolio managers. Technology breakthroughs allow market data vendors such as Telerate, Reuters and Bloomberg to lower the cost and enhance service capabilities and availability of market data for capital and equity markets.

In addition to market-data vendors, some investment software firms have created software systems for complete fixed-income, PC-based workstations. These user-friendly systems are menu-driven and require no special training or computer knowledge to generate sophisticated reports. Analytics can be performed on a single bond or an entire portfolio. Investment managers can perform complete simulation and "what if" analyses. Institutions can review, analyze, and alter portfolios to determine the best strategies to reach investment objectives. Customized reports can be produced for specific management needs to measure duration, convexity, and cash flow.

Some institutions are keeping pace with these technology and portfolio management changes. Other institutions are not. It is important for institutions to learn the new order in investment portfolio management. Statement 115 means the world has changed. Hopefully, Statement 115 will be remembered for the good that it brought to the management of the investment portfolio.

SUMMARY

The advent of Statement 115 marks the beginning of a new era in investment portfolio management. Institutions should not underestimate the difficulty of managing the investment portfolio under Statement 115. Decisions made now with respect to managing the portfolio will have a long-term impact on investment income, liquidity, and control of interest rate risk. Institutions must guard against unnecessarily restricting future investment activities and interest rate risk. The following chapters are designed to help institutions make the strategic decisions required to implement market-value accounting with the goal of having an investment portfolio that is high yielding, marketable, and postured opportunistically against a wider variety of interest rate scenarios.

Chapter 2: Liquidity and Capital at Risk

Table of Contents—

Develop an Investment Plan
Assess Interest Rate Risk and Liquidity Needs
Determine Capital at Risk
  Conflict Between Managing Capital
      and Interest Rate Risk
  Use of Duration to Measure Capital at Risk
  Historical Comparison of Investments and Capital
Impact on Financial Statement Ratios
Summary

The principles of Statement 115 make it important for an institution to accurately measure interest rate risk and adopt an investment plan that will enhance flexibility and maintain earnings stability in a variety of interest rate environments. The interest rate risk posture of an institution should be evaluated on a regular basis to assure that a coordinated and consistent investment management philosophy is being implemented. Liquidity needs should also be forecasted and investment strategies adjusted to accommodate the institution's anticipated funding needs.

    Unfortunately, at many institutions, the investment planning process described above is not being performed. Investment planning at these institutions is too often limited to phone conversations with a bond salesman regarding a new investment product. This dialogue is not enough. Statement 115 adds a new dimension to the investment decision. Institutions must now decide into which category to place an investment—held-to-maturity or available-for-sale. Without performing the investment planning process described above, an institution is ill-prepared to manage the portfolio.

Preliminary indications are that institutions are "taking drastically different tacks toward compliance" with Statement 115. Following are expectations of how various institutions will handle the implementation of Statement 115:

- Wachovia Corporation, a $33 billion-asset bank, headquartered in Winston-Salem, North Carolina, plans to classify 35 percent of its $6.6 billion investment portfolio as available-for-sale primarily for liquidity purposes.

- Banknorth Group, Inc., a $1.6 billion-asset bank, headquartered in Burlington, Vermont, which adopted lower of cost or market (LOCOM) accounting in September 1992, plans to classify its $424 million investment portfolio as available-for-sale and "manage the portfolio closely" to control interest rate risk and reduce capital exposure.

- Coconut Grove Bank, a $280 million-asset bank in Miami, Florida, originally intended to classify its $175 million investment portfolio as held-to-maturity but now expects to classify approximately one-third of its portfolio as available-for-sale.

- First National Bank of Ohio, a $2.2 billion-asset bank in Akron, Ohio, plans to classify its $750 million investment portfolio as available-for-sale to maintain management control of the investment portfolio.

- Taneytown Bank & Trust Company, a $185 million-asset bank in Taneytown, Maryland, despite having a risk-based capital ratio of over 15 percent, plans to classify no more than one-half of its $50 million investment portfolio as available-for-sale to reduce capital at risk.

- The First National Bank of Homestead, a $185 million-asset bank in Homestead, Florida, with a small concentration of agricultural loans, plans to classify most of its $125 million investment portfolio as held-to-maturity, but will classify enough securities in the available-for-sale category to ensure liquidity for seasonal loan demand.

Can these banks be reading from the same accounting rule? The answer is "yes." Classifying the investment portfolio under Statement 115 involves a risk/reward trade-off. Classifying too many securities as available-for-sale could result in too much capital risk. Classifying too few securities as available-for-sale decreases the liquidity of the investment portfolio. Each institution above has evaluated the risk/reward relationship of managing the investment portfolio under Statement 115 and has classified securities to optimize this capital risk/liquidity relationship.

The purpose of Chapter 2, Liquidity and Capital at Risk, is to describe how to "bracket" the amount of securities to be held in the available-for-sale category. Institutions must classify enough securities as available-for-sale to meet liquidity requirements. But, institutions must not classify too many securities as available-for-sale to avoid too much capital at risk.

While risk profiles and management styles may differ, one thing never changes: Thorough planning results in decisions that stand the test of time.

DEVELOP AN INVESTMENT PLAN

Statement 115 provides management with a timely opportunity to upgrade the investment planning process. Initially, institutions must develop a plan to classify the existing investment portfolio. However, this plan for classifying investment securities should become an ongoing part of managing the investment portfolio.

Fundamentally, the goal is simple. Institutions must classify securities as either held-to-maturity or available-for-sale. (The third category, the trading account, is largely unaffected by Statement 115.) But solving the Statement 115 investment classification riddle is not so simple. Perhaps it is because of the permanence of the held-to-maturity classification. Or maybe it is because of the related capital volatility of the available-for-sale category. It seems that the best solution is like choosing between the lesser of two evils, a series of compromises.

To develop an effective investment plan, an institution should determine the overall objective for its investment portfolio. For most institutions this objective is as follows:

- Employ excess customer deposits not needed to meet loan demand;
- Provide liquidity to accommodate deposit and loan fluctuations;
- Secure public and trust deposits; and
- Earn the maximum overall return commensurate with the need for liquidity, taking into consideration interest rate sensitivity, credit quality, and needs of the core institution.

A comprehensive investment plan for managing the portfolio under Statement 115 must be dynamic, not static. The maturity and mix structure of the investment portfolio should be the answer to the question, "How do I optimize the financial performance of the institution given the asset/liability management risk profile of loan and deposit activities?" Since other banking activities are dynamic, investment planning must be dynamic as well.

An investment planning process to be performed in connection with the implementation of Statement 115 is summarized as follows:

1. Assess interest rate risk and liquidity needs considering—

   - Deposit run-off under extreme conditions.
   - Reasonable fluctuations in loan demand.
   - Liquidation of fed funds sold.
   - Access to credit markets, including fed funds purchased.

   See separate section below, Assess Interest Rate Risk and Liquidity Needs, for further analysis.

2. Determine capital at risk resulting from available-for-sale securities. See separate section below, Determine Capital at Risk, for further analysis.

3. Periodically, evaluate the classification of the investment portfolio to be sure that securities are classified in the proper categories. See Chapter 3, Classification of Investment Securities, for further analysis.

4. Periodically conduct a buy/hold/sell evaluation to determine if the reason a security was initially purchased is still valid. If conditions have changed such that the institution would no longer purchase a particular security, then determine the most advantageous way to remedy the situation. See Chapter 4, Managing the Investment Portfolio, for further analysis.

5. Simulate performance of the current investment portfolio in different rate environments (e.g., rising, falling, and flat) to determine price volatility (duration), income return, and cash flow variability under changing prepayments. See Chapter 4 for further analysis.

6. Forecast the change in the net interest margin in a variety of interest rate environments and determine: 1) the extent to which the investment portfolio will be used to adjust or hedge interest rate risk, and 2) the extent that derivative products will be used to adjust or hedge interest rate risk. See Chapter 5, Hedging the Portfolio with Derivatives, for further analysis.

ASSESS INTEREST RATE RISK AND LIQUIDITY NEEDS

This evaluation should be updated periodically in connection with the annual budget or more frequently if warranted. (Statement 115 requires institutions to affirm the classification of investment securities at each reporting date.) The objective of this evaluation is to determine liquidity requirements to be met by the investment portfolio in general and the available-for-sale category in particular. Many institutions currently do this type of evaluation as a traditional liquidity analysis. An example of this analysis is illustrated in Table 2.1, Implied Available-for-Sale Securities.

Table 2.1 approaches the issue of deciding the amount of available-for-sale securities from a "top-down" financial management perspective. This decision is important and should be ratified by executive management of the institution. After determining the total amount of available-for-sale securities in this manner, the portfolio manager should review the existing investment portfolio on a security-by-security basis, or a "bottom-up" approach. As discussed in Chapter 3, Classification of Investment Securities, this bottom-up approach will allow the portfolio manager to choose the best security for the available-for-sale category.

Policy Reserve Requirements discussed in Table 2.1 are liquidity or cash requirements that might be reasonably expected from "normal" banking activities. Estimating Policy Reserve Requirements is a subjective process, based on the institution's knowledge of local market competition, the overall economic outlook, asset/liability management issues, and numerous other considerations. Some examples of Policy Reserve Requirements for loans, deposits, short term assets, and borrowings are illustrated on Table 2.2, Policy Reserve Requirements.

There is a dual purpose in estimating Policy Reserve Requirements. On the one hand, institutions are attempting to estimate funds required under conditions of high loan demand and deposit run-off. Along these lines, institutions should attempt to forecast spikes in loan and deposit balances so that sufficient liquidity is available to fund these activities. In estimating these Policy Reserve Requirements, institutions may wish to use statistical methods such as trendlines, moving averages, or regression analysis.

On the other hand, institutions should attempt to reduce (optimize) the size of the available-for-sale investment category to the minimum required. Along these lines, institutions should forecast probable trends, not disaster scenarios. (The sale of held-to-maturity investments is permissible under Statement

> *"Institutions should perform a comprehensive asset/liability management evaluation to assess interest rate risk and liquidity needs."*

Table 2.1 IMPLIED AVAILABLE-FOR-SALE SECURITIES

	Amount (in millions)	
Policy Reserve Requirements:		
Loans and Commitments—		
Consumer Loans	$ 270	
Revolving Consumer Loans	104	
Commercial Commitments	1,023	
Commercial Loans not Under Lines		
Total Loans and Commitments		$1,775
Deposit Run-off (Excludes Large-denomination CDs)—		
Individual	515	
Public	50	
Other	338	
Total Deposit Run-off		903
Total Policy Reserve Requirements (A)		2,678
Sources of Policy Reserves:		
Liquidate Short-term Assets—		
Fed Funds Sold	964	
Interest-bearing Due from Banks	88	
Total Short-term Asset Sale		1,052
Purchased Funds Capacity—		
Target Maximum Purchased Funds	3,173	
Less Actual Purchased Funds		
Funds Purchased	$ 376	
Foreign Time Deposits	223	
Large-denomination CDs	1,314	
Total Purchased Funds Capacity	1,913	1,260
Total Sources of Funding Reserves (B)		2,312
Implied Available-For-Sale Securities (A)-(B)		366
Adjustments—		
Interest Rate Risk[1]	300	
Capital Cushion[2]	200	
Other[3]	100	
Total Adjustments		600
Actual Available-for-Sale Securities		$ 966

Table 2.1 IMPLIED AVAILABLE-FOR-SALE SECURITIES (cont.)

Footnotes:

1. Interest Rate Risk Represents available-for-sale securities set aside for managing the institutions's interest rate risk position. In this example, the institution is gap neutral from an asset/liability management perspective. However, the institution may wish to become asset sensitive or liability sensitive in which case sufficient securities must be available for sale to manage interest rate risk. This "interest rate risk" adjustment is considered to be a net increase to Implied Available-for-Sale Securities.

2. Capital Cushion This category includes positive or negative "Capital Cushion" adjustments to available-for-sale securities. In this example, due to excellent capital ratios, this institution can accommodate available-for-sale securities in excess of the Implied Available-for-Sale Securities calculated above. Alternatively, due to excessive capital volatility resulting from the market risk of available-for-sale securities, an institution might choose to reduce implied available-for-sale investments. This would require a negative adjustment to the "Capital Cushion."

3. Other This category includes adjustments for current and anticipated issues such as permissible transfers from the held-to-maturity category, tax planning (e.g., purchase of additional municipal securities to take advantage of an expected tax increase), regulatory restrictions (e.g., CMOs that fail the FFIEC stress test), liquidity and other special situations that might warrant higher, or lower, available-for-sale securities.

Table 2.2 POLICY RESERVE REQUIREMENTS

Banking Activity	Example of Policy Reserve Requirement
Loans and commitments	Percent of loan category (e.g., 10%); Percent of total commitments (e.g., 30%)
Deposit run-off	Percent of total deposits (e.g., 15%)
Liquidate fed funds sold	Percent of current short term asset balances (e.g., 75%)
Access to credit markets	Target maximum borrowings less current balances

115 for a variety of reasons including, "other events that are isolated, nonrecurring, and unusual for the reporting enterprise that could not have been reasonably anticipated.") Finally, Table 2.1 can be prepared on a pro forma basis, projecting Policy Reserve Requirements after an acquisition, divestiture, or major banking program.

Many smaller institutions have not formally documented analyses such as Tables 2.1, because they viewed the entire investment portfolio as a liquidity reserve. Depending on how many securities are classified as available-for-sale, this liquidity reserve no longer exists because Statement 115 removes the liquidity safety net. Liquidity analysis will be scrutinized more closely by bank examiners and independent accountants. Institutions should prepare a liquidity analysis similar to Table 2.1 to defend decisions to classify investments.

DETERMINE CAPITAL AT RISK

Statement 115 will have the greatest negative impact on marginally capitalized institutions. Because of FDICIA and other considerations, these institutions cannot afford to "lose" capital due to a decline in the market value of available-for-sale securities. Four factors affect the amount of capital that an institution is at risk to lose:

- The total amount of available-for-sale securities;
- Interest rate risk of these securities;
- Interest rate volatility; and
- Hedges or stop-loss limits, if any.

The following section describes how to measure capital at risk based on the characteristics of the available-for-sale investment portfolio.

Conflict Between Managing Capital and Interest Rate Risk

Statement 115 creates a conflict between managing interest rate risk and managing capital because the investment strategy that is best for managing organizational interest rate risk may expose the institution to intolerable capital risk. This is particularly true for asset-sensitive institutions with large investment portfolios that may need to reduce organizational interest rate risk by extending maturities of the investment portfolio.

In the past, institutions followed primarily a buy-and-hold investment philosophy and accounted for investment securities at amortized cost. Because gains or losses on the investment portfolio, as well as related funding sources, were not marked-to-market, institutions were more willing to purchase long-term investments for the core portfolio. For example, in the early 1980s, municipal securities accounted for approximately 40 percent of an investment portfolio. Most of these were long-term investments that acted as a countercyclical balance to the normal interest rate/credit cycle. Long-term investments provide core earnings during recessionary periods when loan demand is weak. However, long-term securities have greater interest rate risk.

Use of Duration to Measure Capital at Risk

One of the measures of interest rate risk is *duration*. Duration is an index number that measures the interest rate sensitivity of any series of cash flows. It is also a measure of the weighted average term to maturity of all cash flows (principal and interest) of an asset or liability. The concept of duration was originated in 1938 when Frederick R. Macaulay wanted an alternative to the term *to maturity* for measuring the average length of time that an option-free (noncallable) bond investment was outstanding.[3]

Duration is calculated as follows[4]:

1. Calculate the present value of each principal and interest payment (cash flow) of an asset or liability, discounted at a market interest rate.

2. Multiply each present value by the number of payments (expressed in years) from the date of determination to the related payment date.

3. Sum the results.

4. Divide the total by the sum of the present values.

Duration provides an estimate of the time needed to recover the cost of an asset or liability. Therefore, the longer the duration of an asset or a liability, the more sensitive its value will be to changes in interest rates. One of the drawbacks of using duration, especially with longer term investments, is that the reinvestment rate assumption used in the duration calculation can have a dramatic impact on the measure of interest rate sensitivity. In measuring duration, a forecast of the future reinvestment rate is required, which is applied to future cash-flow streams. If this reinvestment rate assumption is too high or too low, then the resulting measure of interest rate sensitivity will be suspect.

"One of the measures of interest rate risk is duration."

> *"Most institutions will choose a risk/reward compromise and classify somewhere between one-third and two-thirds of their investments as available-for-sale."*

Duration analysis can be calculated using different reinvestment rate assumptions with probabilities assigned to each scenario.

As an example, the duration of a ten-year zero coupon bond is 10. The duration of a ten-year U.S. Treasury Note, 5.75 percent coupon, is reduced to 7.37 because of the effect of coupon payments on the duration cash-flow calculations.

The change in price resulting from a change in interest rates of individual securities, as well as for total investment portfolios, can be readily calculated by investment data systems such as Bloomberg. Bloomberg was used to calculate the price change data included in Table 2.3, Illustration of Duration and Capital at Risk[5].

Capital ratios can be calculated for: 1) Risk-based Capital Ratio, 2) Tier I Capital/Risk Based Assets, and 3) Tier I Capital/Total Assets (leverage ratio). The capital ratios presented in Table 2.3 above are illustrated graphically on Figures 2.1, 2.2, and 2.3.

Institutions can use Table 2.3 and Figures 2.1, 2.2, and 2.3 to make a "ball park" estimate of the amount of capital that will be allowed to be "at risk." For example, if an institution: 1) has an investment portfolio with an average maturity of four years or less, 2) wants protection for an increase in interest rates of 300 basis points, 3) wants a capital ratio in excess of 6.88%, then 4) securities classified as available-for-sale cannot exceed two-thirds of the investment portfolio. (See Table 2.3 for 6.88% capital ratio.)

In addition to the above analysis, other factors will affect the amount of securities classified as available-for-sale including the institution's management style, appetite for risk, capitalization ratio and loan portfolio credit quality for which capital may be required. Also, the data in Table 2.3 may be somewhat unrealistic because it was prepared under the assumption that hedges and stop-loss limits were not used. Nonetheless, the Table and Figures illustrate the capital risk that exists with the available-for-sale investment portfolio under different interest rate scenarios.

Most institutions will choose a risk/reward compromise and classify somewhere between one-third and two-thirds of their investments as available-for-sale. This compromise reduces capital at risk and, subject to meeting the liquidity requirements determined in Table 2.1, should provide the institution with ample liquidity. Institutions that classify more than two-thirds, or less than one-third, of the investment portfolio as available-for-sale should be prepared to support their risk/reward investment decision with appropriate documentation and analysis. For example, a decision to classify 100 percent of investments as

Table 2.3 ILLUSTRATION OF DURATION AND CAPITAL AT RISK

Assumptions:

1. $100 million-asset institution.
2. $25 million investment portfolio of U.S. Treasury securities with final maturities of 2, 3, 4, 5 *or* 10 years.
3. $8 million capital.
4. 35 percent corporate income tax rate.

Percentage change in market value of available-for-sale securities under different interest rate scenarios and maturity structures:

Increase In Yield	Decrease in Investment Market Value				
	2 Year	3 Year	4 Year	5 Year	10 Year
Up 100 Basis Points	1.83%	2.67%	3.58%	4.25%	7.37%
Up 200 Basis Points	3.63	5.26	7.01	8.29	14.09
Up 300 Basis Points	5.37	7.76	10.31	12.13	20.23

Using the above percentage decreases in investment market value and the corporate tax rate of 35 percent, pro forma capital ratios are computed for three investment classification scenarios as follows:

Classify One-Third Available-for-Sale, Two-Thirds Held-to-Maturity—

Increase in Yield	Capital Ratios for Different Maturities				
	2 Year	3 Year	4 Year	5 Year	10 Year
Up 100 Basis Points	7.90%	7.83%	7.81%	7.77%	7.60%
Up 200 Basis Points	7.80	7.69	7.62	7.55	7.24
Up 300 Basis Points	7.71	7.56	7.44	7.34	6.90

Classify Two-Thirds Available-for-Sale, One-Third Held-to-Maturity—

Increase in Yield	Capital Ratios for Different Maturities				
	2 Year	3 Year	4 Year	5 Year	10 Year
Up 100 Basis Points	7.80%	7.66%	7.61%	7.54%	7.20%
Up 200 Basis Points	7.61	7.38	7.24	7.10	6.47
Up 300 Basis Points	7.42	7.11	6.88	6.69	5.81

Classify 100% Available-for-Sale, None Held-to-Maturity—

Increase in Yield	Capital Ratios for Different Maturities				
	2 Year	3 Year	4 Year	5 Year	10 Year
Up 100 Basis Points	7.70%	7.50%	7.42%	7.31%	6.80%
Up 200 Basis Points	7.41	7.08	6.86	6.65	5.71
Up 300 Basis Points	7.13	6.67	6.32	6.03	4.71

available-for-sale may be appropriate for a well capitalized institution with an average life of the portfolio of less than two years. Or an institution may have an average maturity in excess of two years but have stop-loss sell orders in place to protect capital if rates increase more than 200 basis points. These and other portfolio management techniques are discussed further in Chapter 4, Managing the Investment Portfolio.

Historical Comparison of Investments and Capital

While the duration analysis presented above is useful, it does not factor into account the real world prospects for interest rate volatility and changing economic cycles. Obviously, if interest rates are stable, the capital at risk is less than if interest rates are volatile. Table 2.4 provides an historical perspective by comparing one institution's investment portfolio gains and losses (net of tax effect) to stockholders' equity from 1970 to 1992.

Figure 2.1 Capital at Risk—Classify One-Third Available-for-Sale

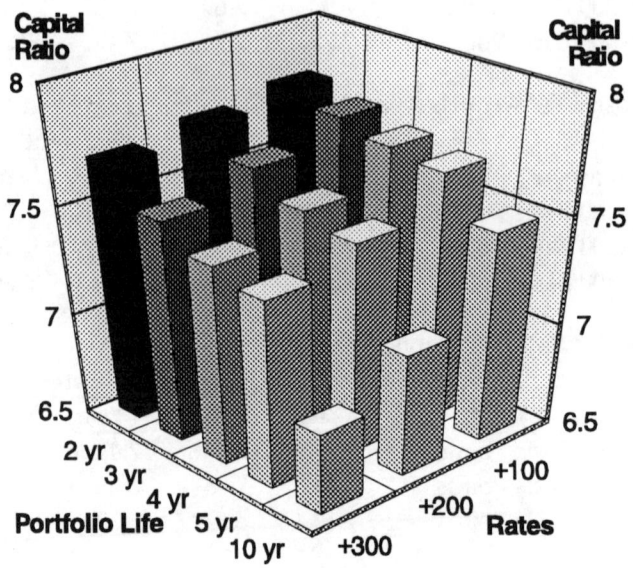

Figure 2.2 Capital at Risk—Classify Two-Thirds Available-for-Sale

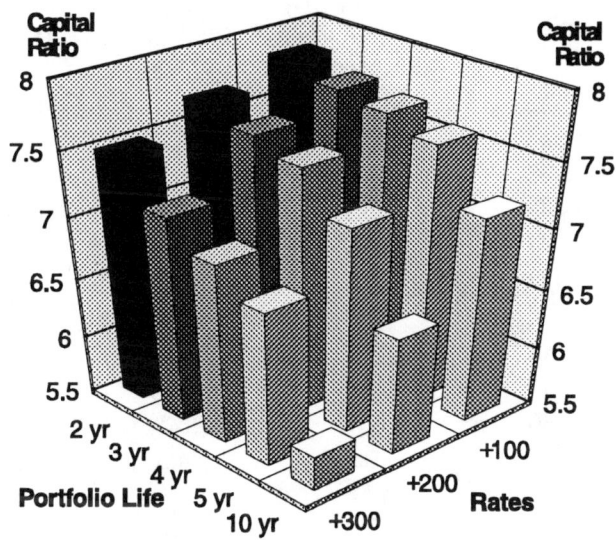

Figure 2.3 Capital at Risk—Classify 100% Available-for-Sale

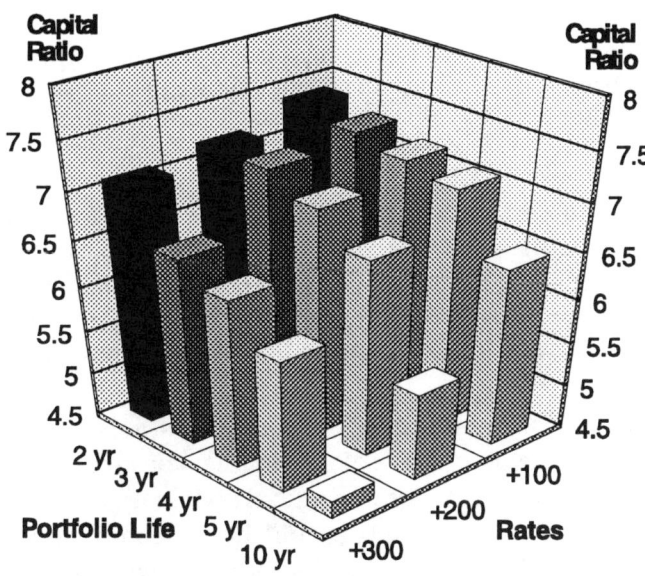

Liquidity and Capital at Risk 21

Table 2.4 Analysis of Investment Market Value and Total Capital

Year	Tax Rate	Investments/ Total Assets	Investment Gain (Loss)*/ Total Capital	Year End Prime Rate
1970	48%	22.0%	(0.2%)	6.75%
1971	48	23.5	1.0	5.25
1972	48	18.7	8.7	6.00
1973	48	17.2	.1	10.00
1974	48	16.1	(7.7)	10.50
1975	48	20.0	(3.5)	7.25
1976	48	17.6	5.0	6.25
1977	48	17.3	2.2	7.75
1978	48	14.2	(3.2)	11.75
1979	46	11.8	(6.5)	15.25
1980	46	12.1	(15.1)	21.50
1981	46	10.5	(14.5)	15.75
1982	46	13.6	3.6	11.50
1983	46	17.0	(0.1)	11.00
1984	46	12.0	1.0	10.75
1985	46	11.6	4.8	9.50
1986	46	12.7	8.9	7.50
1987	40	15.8	1.3	8.75
1988	34	15.2	(0.2)	10.50
1989	34	15.0	4.3	10.50
1990	34	14.4	4.1	10.00
1991	34	18.9	9.3	6.50
1992	34	19.4	7.3	6.00

Source: Investment and capital percentages per Wachovia Corporation financial statements and records, not restated for mergers.
Year end prime rate as set by Wachovia Bank.
* Net of tax effect.

The Investment Gain (Loss)/Total Capital disclosures in Table 2.4 are for the institution's total investment portfolio. In adopting Statement 115, some securities will be classified as held-to-maturity so the pro forma effect of adopting Statement 115 will not be as significant as the capital impact illustrated in Table 2.4.

For example, if one-third of the total investment portfolio were classified as available-for-sale, then the worst capital erosion would have occurred in 1980 and 1981 when approximately 5 percent of stockholders' equity would have been eliminated. Bear in mind that the total investment portfolio was only 10 to 12 percent of total assets during this period compared to nearly

25 percent during the early 1970s and 20 percent in 1992. If high rates occur during a period of high investment balances, the impact could be greater than the worst case indicated above.

IMPACT ON FINANCIAL STATEMENT RATIOS

The following pro forma illustration shows the impact of Statement 115 on certain financial statement ratios.

Table 2.5 Pro Forma Financial Statement Ratios

	Amount (000's omitted)
Pro Forma Investment and Capital Accounts:	
Investment Securities Market Value	$6,950,069
Investment Securities Book Value	6,604,313
Difference	345,756
Assumed Investment Securities Classified as Available-for-Sale	× 35%
Available-for-Sale Market Valuation Account	121,105
Unrealized Gain or Loss Equity Account (net of taxes of 35%)	$ 78,659

Pro Forma Financial Ratios:	As Stated	Pro Forma	Difference
Return on Equity Ratio	17.33%	16.86%	(0.47%)
Tier 1 Capital Ratio	10.06	10.31	0.25
Total Risk Based Capital Ratio	13.34	13.57	0.23
Return on Assets Ratio	1.50	1.50	0.00

Source: Wachovia Corporation financial records as of June 30, 1993.

The most significant impact on the financial statement ratios from adopting Statement 115 will be on the Return on Equity Ratio. If the entire investment portfolio were to be classified as available-for-sale in Table 2.5 above, the Return on Equity Ratio would change from (0.47%) to nearly (1.5%). The Tier I and Total Risk Based Capital Ratios were diluted an average of 24 basis points or approximately 2 percent of total capital. This dilution effect would have been over 6 percent of total capital if all securities were classified as available-for-sale. This dilution could be a problem for a marginally capitalized institution. There was no effect on the return on asset ratio.

Chapter 3, Classification of Investment Securities, includes a mark-to-market worksheet to help the portfolio manager to evaluate "what if" scenarios to measure capital risk related to different available-for-sale portfolios.

SUMMARY

Statement 115 provides management with a timely opportunity to upgrade the investment planning process. Institutions should perform a comprehensive asset/liability management evaluation to assess interest rate risk and liquidity needs of the investment portfolio in general and the available-for-sale category in particular. Solving the Statement 115 investment classification riddle is not simple. It seems that the best solution is like choosing between the lesser of two evils, a series of compromises. Classifying the investment portfolio involves a risk/reward trade-off. Classifying too many securities as available-for-sale could result in too much capital risk. Classifying too few securities as available-for-sale decreases the liquidity of the investment portfolio. Each institution must evaluate this risk/reward relationship to managing the investment portfolio under Statement 115 and classify securities to optimize the financial performance of the investment portfolio. Most institutions will choose a risk/reward compromise and classify somewhere between one-third and two-thirds of their investments as available-for-sale. Institutions that classify more than two-thirds or less than one-third of the investment portfolio as available-for-sale must support their risk/reward investment decision with appropriate documentation and analysis.

ENDNOTES:

1. Steve Cocheo, *ABA Banking Journal*, September 1993, p. 71.

2. Concept of Implied Available-for-Sale Securities developed by James W. Smith, Jr., Wachovia Bank of North Carolina, N.A., at Wachovia Mark-to-Market Investment Conference, August 19,1993.

3. Frederick R. Macaulay, *The Movements of Interest Rates, Bond Yields and Stock Prices in the United States Since 1856* (New York: National Bureau of Economic Research, 1938).

4. John E. Bowen, *Investing in Mortgage Securities, Risks and Rewards for Banks*, Chicago, Bank Administration Institute, 1989, p. 52.

5. Concept of Duration and Capital at Risk developed by Richard B. Roberts, Jr., Wachovia Bank of North Carolina, N.A., at Wachovia Mark-to-Market Investment Conference, August 19, 1993.

Chapter 3: Classification of Investment Securities

Table of Contents—

Investment Philosophy—Buy-and-Hold or Total Return?
Strategies for Classifying Investment Securities
   Held-to-Maturity Classification
   Available-for-Sale Classification
   Product Liquidity Classification
   Barbell Maturity Classification
   Mix and Match by Individual Security Classification
How Much is too Much?
Mark-to-Market Worksheets
Mark-to-Market Worksheet Classification Notes
Investment Classification Recommendations
Gains Trading and Other Financial Management Issues
Summary

Perhaps the most important step in the classification of investment securities is to determine the *total amount* of securities to be held in the available-for-sale category. The process for determining this amount is described in Chapter 2, Liquidity and Capital at Risk. Institutions must classify enough securities as available-for-sale to meet forward funding (liquidity) requirements. But, institutions must not classify too many securities as available-for-sale because of related capital risk.

After an institution has determined the approximate size of the available-for-sale category, the process of choosing individual securities for this category becomes somewhat easier. There are no absolute rules for classifying securities—most securities will perform well in either category. Chapter 2 described why most institutions should classify between one-third and two-thirds of total investment securities as available-for-sale. Chapter 3 describes several methodologies for choosing securities for the available-for-sale category. In addition, Chapter 3 includes a Mark-to-Market Worksheet to help the portfolio manager evaluate "what-if" scenarios to measure capital risk related to different available-for-sale portfolios. Recommendations on the classification of specific investment products are included at the end of this chapter.

INVESTMENT PHILOSOPHY—BUY-AND-HOLD OR TOTAL RETURN?

Before undertaking the classification of investment securities, the institution should evaluate its intentions for managing the available-for-sale category. The decision of how an institution will manage the available-for-sale category will have a direct impact on the choice of securities for this category. Specifically, there are two opposing investment management philosophies on how to manage the available-for-sale category, which are summarized as follows:

- *Buy-and-Hold* investment management, whereby securities are placed in the available-for-sale category and, except for permissible sales (or transfers) such as a significant deterioration in the issuer's creditworthiness, are held to maturity. See Chapter 4, Managing the Investment Portfolio for further description.

- *Total Return* investment management, whereby securities are placed in the available-for-sale category and managed closely, employing stop-loss sell orders, hedges, and other strategies to enhance investment performance, control interest rate risk, and protect capital. See Chapter 4, Managing the Investment Portfolio for further description.

Each institution is different. Some institutions are not comfortable with the total return investment philosophy. Other institutions have never held a bond to maturity. This bias will affect the classification of investment securities. For example, an institution that has traditionally been a buy-and-hold investor would probably be most comfortable with a relatively large held-to-maturity category. On the other hand, an institution that is prone to actively manage the investment portfolio through swaps and total return strategies would probably be most comfortable with a relatively large available-for-sale category. Some institutions are in between, using both the buy-and-hold and total return philosophies for different portions of the investment portfolio.

The accounting changes of Statement 115 are quite significant and an institution may wish to re-evaluate its overall investment management practices. Is the institution alert to total return strategies? Has the institution purchased a bond analytics sys-

"Some institutions are not comfortable with the total return investment philosophy."

tem such as Bloomberg? Is the investment portfolio up-to-date for new investment products, accounting systems, etc? The advent of Statement 115 does not mean that an institution must embrace a totally new investment management philosophy. Changes in investment management, if any, should be evolutionary, not revolutionary.

Individual securities targeted for the available-for-sale category should be analyzed based on *expected* total return performance since these securities will be accounted for on a mark-to-market basis. This performance analysis may affect an institution's intent, ability, or desire to hold a particular security in either the available-for-sale or held-to-maturity categories.

STRATEGIES FOR CLASSIFYING INVESTMENT SECURITIES

There are probably as many ways to classify the existing investment portfolio as there are securities in the portfolio. Institutions have struggled so much with the classification of the investment portfolio that even swap strategies and derivatives seem tame by comparison. Five different investment classification strategies are described below. These investment management strategies are discussed further in Chapter 4, Managing the Investment Portfolio.

Held-to-Maturity Classification

Under this strategy, the institution would classify most or all of the investment portfolio as held-to-maturity. The institution would follow a buy-and-hold investment management philosophy. Investment accounting would continue on the amortized cost basis.

Advantages—

- More traditional approach.
- No capital volatility.
- Can ignore market volatility.
- Reduces time required to manage portfolio.

Disadvantages—

- Regulators probably will not approve.
- Investment portfolio not up-to-date for new trends, products, and strategies.
- Prohibits active liquidity management.

- Limits flexibility to effectively manage in uncertain environment.
- More difficult to manage interest rate risk through the investment portfolio.
- Investment swaps not possible.
- CMOs that fail the "high-risk" test could "taint" other CMOs.

Recommendation—

- Possible strategy for institutions that have buy-and-hold track record.
- Defensive strategy for marginally capitalized institutions.

A typical held-to-maturity investment portfolio would be classified as follows:

Available-for-Sale	Held-to-Maturity
• None	• Treasuries and Agencies
	• CMOs
	• MBS—ARMs
	• MBS—Fixed Rate
	• Tax-exempts
	• Corporates and Other

Available-for-Sale Classification

Under this strategy, the institution would classify most or all of the investment portfolio as available-for-sale. The institution would follow more of a total return investment management philosophy. Gains and losses on the investment portfolio would be marked-to-market through a valuation reserve reported in shareholders' equity.

Advantages—

- Maximum investment flexibility.
- Maximum investment liquidity.

Disadvantages—

- Capital volatility.
- Continuous buy/sell/hold decisions require more demanding investment management, including access to current bond market data.
- May encourage smaller portfolio and shorter average lives to mitigate capital risk.

Recommendation—
- Possible strategy for well capitalized institutions.
- Smaller institutions adopting this strategy may require independent portfolio advisor for expertise.

A typical available-for-sale investment portfolio would be classified as follows:

Available-for-Sale	Held-to-Maturity
• Treasuries and Agencies	• None
• CMOs	
• MBS—ARMs	
• MBS—Fixed Rate	
• Tax-exempts	
• Corporates and Other	

Product Liquidity Classification

Under this strategy, the institution would concentrate on preserving liquidity in the available-for-sale category. The most liquid investment products (e.g., Treasuries, Agencies, etc.) would be classified as available-for-sale to fund Policy Reserves Requirements described in Chapter 2, Liquidity and Capital at Risk. Remaining investments would be classified as held-to-maturity.

Advantages—
- Easy to understand.
- Liquidity emphasis of available-for-sale category is congruent with primary objective of investment portfolio.
- Retains amortized cost accounting for more volatile securities in held-to-maturity category.
- Capability to shorten or lengthen average life of both categories depending upon market conditions and liquidity needs.

Disadvantages—
- Rigid categories may restrict market opportunities.
- Not evaluating the true risk/reward of investments.
- More volatile assets tend to remain in held-to-maturity, which could exacerbate long-term earnings volatility.

> *"The duration of each category can be modified based on the institution's interest rate outlook and liquidity needs."*

Recommendation—

- Systematic approach for buy-and-hold institutions, providing liquidity in available-for-sale portfolio as needed.

A typical product liquidity investment portfolio would be classified as follows:

Available-for-Sale
(Most likely to sell)
- Treasuries and Agencies
- CMOs
- MBS—ARMs

Held-to-Maturity
(Least likely to sell)
- MBS—Fixed Rate
- Tax-exempts
- Corporates and Other

Barbell Maturity Classification

Under this strategy, the institution would classify investment securities based on the duration of investments. Short-term (e.g., less than two years) securities would be classified as available-for-sale to satisfy liquidity needs. Long-term securities would be classified in the held-to-maturity category as core investments. The duration of each category can be modified based on the institution's interest rate outlook and liquidity needs. For example, if an institution is somewhat bearish on the bond market, the portfolio manager may want to purchase short-term investments for the available-for-sale category. Alternatively, if an institution is bullish on the bond market, the portfolio manager may want to purchase long-term investments for the held-to-maturity category.

Advantages—

- Short-term, more-liquid securities in available-for-sale category results in market price stability, which minimizes capital loss.
- Strategy can be employed selectively when market conditions (e.g., positively sloped yield curve) or interest rate outlook warrants.

Disadvantages—

- Must hold long-term maturities to maturity.
- The potential gains in the investment portfolio will tend to be concentrated in the held-to-maturity account where securities most likely to increase in value (i.e., highest duration) are held.
- May not properly consider liquidity needs.
- MBS prepayments further complicate liquidity management.

Recommendation—

- Good strategy for institutions wishing to manage interest rate risk in the investment portfolio while minimizing capital risk.

A typical barbell maturity investment portfolio would be classified as follows:

Available-for-Sale
(e.g., under two years maturity)
- Treasuries and Agencies
- CMOs
- MBS—ARMs
- MBS—Fixed Rate
- Tax-exempts
- Corporates and Other

Held-to-Maturity
(e.g., over two years maturity)
- Treasuries and Agencies
- CMOs
- MBS—ARMs
- MBS—Fixed Rate
- Tax-exempts

Mix and Match by Individual Security Classification

Under this strategy, the institution would classify investment securities based upon a combination of strategies. After evaluating the various classification strategies described above, the institution may decide that none of these singular strategies fulfills its investment goals and objectives. Individual securities would be classified independently in order to achieve liquidity and capital risk goals.

Advantages—

- Allows active management of market volatility associated with selected securities and special situations.

- Available-for-sale category can be structured so that certain securities perform better if rates rise (e.g., ARMs) whereas other securities perform better if rates fall (e.g., three year Treasuries).

Disadvantages—

- Managing available-for-sale and held-to-maturity categories could become unwieldy without consistent investment plan.

- Value analysis may change in different interest rate environment.

- Subjective, hard to defend.

Recommendation—

- Good strategy for diversified portfolios, which may not fit any other classification strategy.

A typical mix and match investment portfolio would be classified as follows:

Available-for-Sale
- Most liquid.
- Shorter duration.
- Closest to break-even.
- Losers that might be sold.
- Most liquid CMOs (PACs, TACs, 1st tranche, etc.).
- Other municipals.

Held-to-Maturity
- Least liquid.
- Longer duration.
- Biggest gains.
- Winners that should not be sold.
- Least liquid CMOs (sequentials, broken PACs, TACs).
- TEFRA-advantaged and CRA-related municipals.

Be aware that bank examiners and independent accountants may not allow certain CMOs to be classified in the held-to-maturity category.

A more detailed discussion of specific securities to be included in each category is included in the Mark-to-Market Classification Notes section below.

HOW MUCH IS TOO MUCH?

After individual securities have been selected for the held-to-maturity or available-for-sale categories, the portfolio manager should ask the question, "Does the investment portfolio achieve the objectives of providing adequate liquidity while minimizing capital risk?" Liquidity requirements for the available-for-sale portfolio were determined in Chapter 2 based on Policy Reserve Requirements.

The next step in Chapter 3 is to measure the capital risk for the investments chosen for the available-for-sale category. This risk must be measured periodically to ensure that capital risk is not in excess of guidelines determined in Chapter 2, Liquidity and Capital Risk. Worded differently, institutions need a way to answer the following question about investments in the available-for-sale category, "How much is too much?"

MARK-TO-MARKET WORKSHEETS

Capital risk created by the classification of the available-for-sale category can be measured using duration and interest sensitivity concepts. The methodology illustrated on the following *Mark-to-Market Worksheets* allows an institution to measure both pro forma capital risk and capital ratios resulting from securities in the available-for-sale category. This worksheet can be prepared annually or at each reporting date if liquidity needs or the interest rate environment change significantly. The Mark-to-Market Worksheet can be modeled easily using spreadsheet software to help the portfolio manager evaluate "what-if" scenarios to measure capital risk related to different available-for-sale portfolios. This allows the institution to structure the optimum classification and size of the available-for-sale category.

The assumptions of Table 3.1, Mark-to-Market Worksheet 100 percent Available-for-Sale[1] is that Forgotten Asset Sate Bank (FASB) has $500 million in total assets and $100 million in the investment portfolio, 100 percent of which is classified in the available-for-sale category. Table 3.1 illustrates the impact of changes in interest rates (e.g., +100 basis points, +200 basis points, and +300 basis points) on the market value of investments and the related impact on capital. Table 3.2 (one-third available-for-sale) and Table 3.3 (two-thirds available-for-sale) illustrate pro forma ratios for smaller available-for-sale portfolios assuming the same duration measures. In reality, these duration measures will be different based upon the specific securities included in an available-for-sale portfolio.

The duration measures for entire portfolios, or classes, of securities such as Treasuries, Agencies, Tax-exempts, CMOs, etc., illustrated on the Mark-to-Market Worksheets are extremely important for the management of the investment portfolio. Investment accounting systems should produce this information on a monthly basis. Otherwise, portfolio managers are faced with the daunting task of obtaining this data on a bond-by-bond basis. The availability of duration measures for entire portfolios should be an important requirement of an investment accounting system.

Table 3.1 Mark-to-Market—100% Available-for-Sale

Forgotten Asset State Bank (FASB)
December 31, 1993

(Amounts in 000s)

Note	Duration	Description	Investment Book Value	−100bp	Current	+100bp	+200bp	+300bp
						Mark-to-Market Gain (Loss)		
A	2.0	Treasuries	$40,000	$1,600	$800	$0	($800)	($1,600)
B	2.0	Agencies	10,000	400	200	0	(200)	(400)
C	5.0	Tax-exempts	10,000	900	400	(100)	(600)	(1,100)
D	3.0	CMOs	10,000	500	200	(100)	(400)	(700)
E	1.0	MBS Arms	5,000	150	100	50	0	(50)
F	4.0	MBS Fixed-rate	20,000	1,200	400	(400)	(1,200)	(2,000)
G	1.0	Corporate and Other	5,000	150	100	50	0	(50)
	2.5	TOTALS	$100,000	$4,900	$2,200	($500)	($3,200)	($5,900)
		Gain (Loss), Percent Change		2.7%	--	-2.7%	-5.4%	-8.1%
		Gain (Loss), Net of Tax of 35%		$3,185	$1,430	($325)	($2,080)	($3,835)

Capital Structure	Capital	−100bp	Current	+100bp	+200bp	+300bp
			Mark-to-Market Capital Increase (Erosion)			
Tier I Capital	$30,000	10.6%	4.8%	-1.1%	-6.9%	-12.8%
Tier I and II Capital	35,000	9.1%	4.1%	-0.9%	-5.9%	-11.0%
Risk Based Assets	350,000					
Total Assets	500,000					

	Minimum Capital Ratios							
Note		Capital Ratio	Book Value	−100bp	Current	+100bp	+200bp	+300bp
				Capital Ratios Adjusted for Gain (Loss), Net of Tax				
H	10.00%	Tier I and II/Risk Based Assets	10.00%	10.91%	10.41%	9.91%	9.41%	8.90%
H	6.00%	Tier I/Risk Based Assets	8.57%	9.48%	8.98%	8.48%	7.98%	7.48%
H	5.00%	Tier I/Total Assets	6.00%	6.64%	6.29%	5.94%	5.58%	5.23%

34 Chapter 3

Table 3.2 Mark-to-Market—One-Third Available-for-Sale

Forgotten Asset State Bank (FASB)
December 31, 1993

(Amounts in 000s)

Note	Duration	Description	Investment Book Value	−100bp	Current	+100bp	+200bp	+300bp
A	2.0	Treasuries	$13,333	$533	$267	$0	($267)	($533)
B	2.0	Agencies	3,333	133	67	0	(67)	(133)
C	5.0	Tax-exempts	3,333	300	133	(33)	(200)	(367)
D	3.0	CMOs	3,333	167	67	(33)	(133)	(233)
E	1.0	MBS Arms	1,667	50	33	17	0	(17)
F	4.0	MBS Fixed-rate	6,667	400	133	(133)	(400)	(667)
G	1.0	Corporate and Other	1,667	50	33	17	0	(17)
	2.5	TOTALS	$33,333	$1,633	$733	($167)	($1,067)	($1,967)

Gain (Loss), Percent Change: 2.7% — −2.7% −5.4% −8.1%

Gain (Loss), Net of Tax of 35%: $1,062 $477 ($108) ($693) ($1,278)

Mark-to-Market Capital Increase (Erosion)

Capital Structure	Capital	−100bp	Current	+100bp	+200bp	+300bp
Tier I Capital	$30,000	3.5%	1.6%	−0.4%	−2.3%	−4.3%
Tier I and II Capital	35,000	3.0%	1.4%	−0.3%	−2.0%	−3.7%
Risk Based Assets	350,000					
Total Assets	500,000					

Capital Ratios Adjusted for Gain (Loss), Net of Tax

Note	Minimum Capital Ratios	Capital Ratio	Book Value	−100bp	Current	+100bp	+200bp	+300bp
H	10.00%	Tier I and II/Risk Based Assets	10.00%	10.30%	10.14%	9.97%	9.80%	9.63%
H	6.00%	Tier I/Risk Based Assets	8.57%	8.87%	8.71%	8.54%	8.37%	8.21%
H	5.00%	Tier I/Total Assets	6.00%	6.21%	6.10%	5.98%	5.86%	5.74%

Table 3.3 Mark-to-Market—Two-Thirds Available-for-Sale

Forgotten Asset State Bank (FASB)
December 31, 1993

(Amounts in 000s)

Note	Duration	Description	Investment Book Value	−100bp	Current	Mark-to-Market Gain (Loss) +100bp	+200bp	+300bp
A	2.0	Treasuries	$26,667	$1,067	$533	$0	($533)	($1,067)
B	2.0	Agencies	6,667	267	133	0	(133)	(267)
C	5.0	Tax-exempts	6,667	600	267	(67)	(400)	(733)
D	3.0	CMOs	6,667	333	133	(67)	(267)	(467)
E	1.0	MBS Arms	3,333	100	67	33	0	(33)
F	4.0	MBS Fixed-rate	13,333	800	267	(267)	(800)	(1,333)
G	1.0	Corporate and Other	3,333	100	67	33	0	(33)
	2.7	TOTALS	$66,667	$3,267	$1,467	($333)	($2,133)	($3,933)

Gain (Loss), Percent Change   2.7%   —   −2.7%   −5.4%   −8.1%

Gain (Loss), Net of Tax of 35% $2,123 $953   ($217)   ($1,387)   ($2,557)

Capital Structure	Capital	−100bp	Current	Mark-to-Market Capital Increase (Erosion) +100bp	+200bp	+300bp
Tier I Capital	$30,000	7.1%	3.2%	−0.7%	−4.6%	−8.5%
Tier I and II Capital	35,000	6.1%	2.7%	−0.6%	−4.0%	−7.3%
Risk Based Assets	350,000					
Total Assets	500,000					

Note	Minimum Capital Ratios	Capital Ratio	Book Value	−100bp	Capital Ratios Adjusted for Gain (Loss), Net of Tax Current	+100bp	+200bp	+300bp
H	10.00%	Tier I and II/Risk Based Assets	10.00%	10.61%	10.27%	9.94%	9.60%	9.27%
H	6.00%	Tier I/Risk Based Assets	8.57%	9.18%	8.84%	8.51%	8.18%	7.84%
H	5.00%	Tier I/Total Assets	6.00%	6.42%	6.19%	5.96%	5.72%	5.49%

36 Chapter 3

MARK-TO-MARKET WORKSHEET CLASSIFICATION NOTES

NOTE A—Treasuries Securities

The duration of the Treasuries portfolio in this illustration is two, which means that a 100 basis point change in interest rates results in a 2 percent change in market value.

Most institutions view Treasuries as the first source of liquidity from the investment portfolio. Therefore, most Treasuries should be included in the available-for-sale category. An exception to this is that many institution will include Treasuries required for deposit-pledging purposes in the held-to-maturity category. In addition, Treasuries may be classified in the held-to-maturity category for specific investment strategies such as for the long end of a "barbell" investment program.

The price changes shown in the Mark-to-Market Worksheets assume an immediate and parallel shift in the yield curve of -100 basis points and +100, +200, and +300 basis points. It is somewhat unlikely to expect an immediate and parallel yield curve shift of 100, 200, or 300 basis points. Therefore, the duration-suggested price increases and decreases are greater than would occur from a gradual rise in interest rates.

For example, as shown in Chapter 2, Table 2.3, the price decrease of a five-year Treasury is 12.13 percent based on an immediate 300 basis point rise in rates. However, if this rate increase occurred over a one year period of time, and the price decline were measured one year from now, the price decrease would be 10.31 percent. This reduction occurs because the security has rolled down the yield curve and is now a four-year Treasury. Therefore, the price projections on the Mark-to-Market Worksheets for Treasuries are worst case scenarios. Along these lines, institutions may wish to choose the 200 basis point change in interest rates column on the Mark-to-Market Worksheets as a more likely worst case scenario for capital risk. This would allow for a larger available-for-sale category for a given mark-to-market capital risk tolerance. The increased risk of a larger available-for-sale category can be mitigated if the institution is prepared to take stop loss action (e.g., sell securities) if interest rates rise 200 basis points. (See Chapter 4, Managing the Investment Portfolio, for further discussion.)

NOTE B—Agencies Securities

The duration of the Agencies portfolio in this illustration is 2 which means that a 100 basis point change in interest rates results in a two percent change in market value.

Agency securities with a fixed rate and stated term maturity structure (i.e., "bullets") should be evaluated similar to Treasuries for investment classification purposes.

An assumption for this illustration is that the Agencies portfolio does not include any of the structured debt securities (e.g., putable or callable bonds, or bonds with other embedded options or swaps) issued by U.S. Government Agencies. It is beyond the scope of this book to describe the price sensitivity of these securities in detail. However, some of the issues to be considered in evaluating these structures for classification purposes include the following:

- *Callable bonds*—Callable bonds have an embedded call option such that if interest rates fall sufficiently, the issuer will call the bond. However, if rates rise, the bond will likely not be called. (For the investor this is a "heads you win, tails I lose" proposition; for the issuer, it is cheap funding.) Thus, callable bonds have limited upside gain potential, but have downside loss potential similar to a noncallable bond. In a falling rate environment, the duration of a callable bond never gets much above one or two, depending upon how much the call price is in or out of the money. Another way to think of this is that since duration is a measure of the weighted average term to maturity of a bond's cash flows, the duration of a callable bond is limited by the time to the next call. However, in a rising rate environment, the duration of a callable bond behaves more like a noncallable bond. Because there is more downside loss potential than upside gain potential, and to protect capital, it may be better to classify callable bonds in the held-to-maturity category rather than the available-for-sale portfolio.

- *Putable Bonds*—Putable bonds have an embedded put option so that if interest rates rise sufficiently, the investor can put the bond back to the issuer. However, if rates fall, the investor will keep the higher yield. (For the investor this is a "heads I win, tails you lose" proposition; for the issuer, it is expensive funding.) Thus, put bonds have limited downside loss potential but have upside gain potential similar to a noncallable bond. Therefore, putable bonds are excellent bonds for the available-for-sale category.

- *Step-up bonds*—Step-up bonds pay a fixed coupon for a year or two until the step-up date at which time the coupon increases, generally one to two percent, to the step-up rate, which will be paid until the bond is called (most step-ups are continuously callable) or until maturity if there is a one-time call at the step-up date. Step-up bonds have limited upside gain potential because, if rates fall (or even rise a little), the bond is structured to be called. If interest rates rise beyond the step-up rate, the bond won't be called but it will trade at a loss. Similar to callable bonds, to protect capital, it may be better to classify step-up bonds in the held-to-maturity category rather than the available-for-sale category.

- *Index amortizing notes (IANs)*—Index amortizing notes are structures with an embedded interest rate swap. After an initial lockout period, IANs follow a principal amortization schedule that is clearly defined in the debenture by the level of an index such as 3-month LIBOR. IANs behave similar to fixed-rate MBS because if the index rate rises, principal amortization (prepayments) slow down and if the index falls, prepayments increase. The price sensitivity of IANs is similar to fixed-rate MBS whereby the prepayment of principal limits price appreciation while extension risk magnifies price decreases. Because of this price sensitivity, it may be better to classify IANs in the held-to-maturity category rather than the available-for-sale portfolio to protect capital.

- *Formula floaters*—Formula floaters are floating-rate securities in which the floating-rate index rate is a long term rate, usually a Constant Maturity Treasury (CMT) rate of 1 to 10 years. Examples of formula floaters would include the following: 1) CMT floater with a coupon rate of the 5-year CMT less 170 basis points, 2) CMT floater with a coupon rate of the 1-year CMT plus 28 basis points with a 200 basis point periodic cap and floor, or 3) CMT floater with a coupon rate of 50 percent of the 10-year CMT plus 125 basis points with a floor of 4.5 percent. Formula floaters are designed to allow investors to exploit the steepness of the yield curve or make a play on the shape of the yield curve. However, if the yield curve flattens or rises, these bonds will trade at a loss.

For classification purposes, formula floaters should be classified in the held-to-maturity category. They have two strikes against them: 1) they have relatively high price volatility potential which results in excessive capital risk, and 2) they don't provide much liquidity in the available-for-sale portfolio because they are "story bonds" which are securities that require a long "story" to sell.

Be aware that bank examiners and independent accountants may not allow certain structured debt securities to be classified in the held-to-maturity category.

NOTE C—Tax-exempt Securities

The duration of the Tax-exempt portfolio in this illustration is 5, which means that a 100 basis point change in interest rates results in a 5 percent change in market value. Tax-exempt bonds frequently have call features that must be considered in the duration calculation. (See above for discussion of call options).

Most institutions will place TEFRA-advantaged and Community Reinvestment Act (CRA)-type tax-exempt securities in the held-to-maturity category because of the strong probability that these securities will be the last resort for liquidity from the investment portfolio. Other municipals can be placed in either the available-for-sale or held-to-maturity categories, depending upon liquidity and capital risk issues.

Insured issues rated AAA are the most liquid tax-exempt security and this liquidity would probably have the most value if classified in the available-for-sale category. On the other hand, nonrated and low-rated tax-exempt securities should be included in the held-to-maturity category because if ratings become a problem in the future, transfers to available-for-sale are permissible. Generally, institutions will tend to place all tax-exempt securities in the held-to-maturity category. However, it may be prudent to classify some as available-for-sale to increase flexibility in the event that an institution has a problem with the Alternative Minimum Tax.

NOTE D—CMOs

The duration of the collateralized mortgage obligation (CMOs) portfolio in this illustration is 3, which means that a 100 basis point change in interest rates results in a 3 percent change in market value.

There are thousands of tranches of CMOs and dozens of structures (e.g., PACs, TACs, VADMs, sequentials, liquidity, supports, floaters, Zs, etc.). Some CMOs are defined as "high risk" by FFIEC if, due to an immediate and parallel shift in the yield curve of plus or minus 300 basis points, any of the following occur: 1) initial weighted average life exceeds 10 years, 2) weighted average life shortens by more than six years or extends by more than four years, or 3) price changes by more than 17 percent. CMOs classified as "high risk" by this stress test should be included in the available-for-sale or trading categories pending the issuance of final guidelines regarding the adoption of Statement 115 by bank regulators.

Institutions must continue to monitor CMOs because some CMOs may initially pass the stress test but subsequently fail because of changes in prepayments. CMOs placed in the held-to-maturity category that subsequently fail the stress test may jeopardize the classification of CMOs remaining in this category depending upon the approach taken by bank examiners and independent accountants. Therefore, CMOs on the verge of failing the FFIEC "high risk" test should not be placed in the held-to-maturity category. Conditions under which a CMO could subsequently fail the stress test include:

- An average life that is very close to any one of the thresholds (4, 6 or 10 years) and that would fail the stress test with a small change in prepayment rates.

- "Barbell" or other unusual cash flow structures that, for example, have high cash flows in the first six months, and, absent these high initial cash flows, the average life extends beyond 10 years. In fact, some CMOs are purposely designed in such a way that they will pass the stress test initially but will fail a few months after being tested. To identify these "barbell" type CMOs, investors should examine cash flow projections, including graphic illustrations, before buying the security.

- Floaters with coupons near the life cap. If a floater caps out, it becomes a fixed-rate CMO and is subject to tests 1) and 2) above in addition to test 3).

- Floaters with extended repricing intervals (i.e., more than one year).

Another effective test to screen for potential "high-risk" CMOs is to assume that interest rates have already moved up or down 100 to 200 basis points and re-run the stress test from the pro forma interest rate levels. This analysis will help identify CMOs that pass the stress test today but may fail next year after interest rates have changed.

The effort described above of identifying potential "high-risk" CMOs and including these in the available-for-sale category does not necessarily mean that the best CMOs (e.g., highly liquid, well-structured PACs, TACs, etc.) should be placed in the held-to-maturity category. It may not be worthwhile to pay a premium for the highly liquid CMOs and then hold these securities to maturity. The added liquidity of a PAC CMO has limited value to an institution if it can't be sold.

Along these lines, it would be better to include the best sequential CMOs, which have less liquidity and higher spreads compared to PAC CMOs, in the held-to-maturity category and include PACs in the available-for-sale category where the added liquidity can be tapped if needed. In addition to liquidity benefits, PACs have price stability under most interest rate scenarios so they are a defensive choice for the available-for-sale category from a capital risk viewpoint.

Many institutions will decide to classify all CMOs as available-for-sale to enhance investment liquidity and keep control over the management of the CMO portfolio. Institutions should discuss their intentions and concerns with bank examiners and independent accountants for assistance in making this and other classification decisions. Bank examiners and independent accountants are responsible for testing compliance with Statement 115 and they should be involved up front with major classification issues. Bank examiners are expected to issue guidance on the use of stress tests in connection with Statement 115 in the fourth quarter 1993.

NOTE E—MBS ARMs

The duration of the adjustable rate mortgage securities (MBS ARMs) portfolio in this illustration is 1, which means that a 100 basis point change in interest rates results in a 1 percent change in market value.

MBS ARMs have a coupon that floats at a fixed margin over a floating index rate. Since ARMs do not have a constant coupon, duration is somewhat limited as a price sensitivity measure. The price sensitivity of ARMs is dependent upon both the coupon rate and the cap (lifetime and annual) rates. Bond analytics systems measure the *option-adjusted spread* (OAS) duration, which considers the pricing of caps in the duration of an ARM. The OAS duration of ARMs is lowest (near zero) for certain FNMA ARMs (e.g., 2 percent annual cap, high lifetime cap, premium price) and is over 3 for certain GNMA ARMs (e.g., 1 percent annual cap, low lifetime cap, discount price). Generally, low OAS duration ARMs with less price sensitivity should be placed in the available-for-sale category for defensive purposes to avoid mark-to-market capital risk. High OAS duration ARMs should be placed in the held-to-maturity category where mark-to-market gains and losses are *not* recorded in the financial statements beyond footnote disclosure. The only downside to this treatment is that institutions should not place too many low cap instruments in the held-to-maturity category. On the other hand, a "low" lifetime cap rate would still be in excess of 9 percent. How many institutions would have a real problem with this interest rate for thirty years?

NOTE F—MBS Fixed Rate Securities

The duration of the fixed rate mortgage-backed securities (MBS) portfolio in this illustration is 4, which means that a 100 basis point change in interest rates results in a 4 percent change in market value.

Unlike CMOs, pass-through MBS (fixed or adjustable rate) do not currently require a FFIEC "high-risk" test. Nonetheless, MBS do have considerable prepayment risk and bond analytics systems have been developed to measure price sensitivity and duration. Duration measurements for MBS are somewhat useful during periods of time when interest rates are relatively stable. However, if interest rates change by more than 1 or 2 percent, as experienced in the early 1990s, then duration is not a good measure of price sensitivity. To begin with, the duration price sensitivity measure is most accurate for changes in interest rates of 1 percent or less. Secondly, the embedded option of mortgage prepayments gives MBS negative convexity, which causes the price of a bond to go down more in a bear market than it goes up in a bull market. Finally, if mortgage prepayments increase or decrease beyond the speed assumptions in the original duration calculation, actual duration may be considerably different from original estimates. Despite these shortcomings, duration is the most widely used measure of price sensitivity of MBS.

At this stage of the interest rate cycle (mortgage rates are the lowest in over 20 years) the biggest concern about MBS is that prepayment speeds will slow, extending the average lives of MBS, with the investor holding a longer term security in a higher rate environment. Higher coupon MBS have a lower duration and are less subject to price volatility and extension risk; lower coupon MBS have a higher duration and are more subject to price volatility and extension risk. Along these lines, it may be better to place high duration MBS in the held-to-maturity category and place low duration MBS in the available-for-sale category.

However, this classification decision is not quite so simple. The portfolio manager cannot necessarily conclude, for example, that all 30-year GNMA 9.0 percents should be classified in the available-for-sale category for reasons described in the following paragraphs.

Complicating matters for the portfolio manager is "book value" accounting on the income statement. With all the emphasis of Statement 115 on mark-to-market, the importance of the book value of a security is often overlooked. Book value drives the income statement for both the available-for-sale and held-to-maturity categories. Understanding how book value affects the yield on investments can help the portfolio manager do a better job of classifying the investment portfolio.

For example, an institution that owns a 30-year GNMA 9.0 percent at par has a security that is quite different *from an income statement perspective* compared to a GNMA 9.0 percent with a book value of 108. The market value of each security is the same. However, a GNMA 9.0 percent owned at par yields 9.0 percent whereas a GNMA 9.0 percent owned at 108 may have a yield of 6.75 percent. In fact, a GNMA 9.0 percent owned at 108 really has more of a "variable yield" because the ultimate book yield depends on prepayment experience. A *9.0 percent fixed yield* and a *6.75 percent variable yield* are quite different investments, and accordingly, the classification of these securities could be different as well.

In fact, the most important issue in this GNMA 9.0 percent illustration may be the investment gain, which may benefit the institution most if this security were placed in the available-for-sale category. Even if the security is a "keeper," and the institution intends to hold it to maturity, it would be nice to start out under Statement 115 with some gains to protect capital with a cushion.

NOTE G—Corporate and Other Securities

The duration of the Corporate and Other portfolio in this illustration is 1, which means that a 100 basis point change in interest rates results in a 1 percent change in market value.

Generally, institutions have less than 5 percent of total investments in other bonds, notes, and debentures, which would include corporate debt securities, bank notes, deposit notes, private label CMOs, etc. Institutions have traditionally purchased these securities as a buy-and-hold earning asset to augment loan demand. Accordingly, these securities should probably be included in the held-to-maturity category.

NOTE H—CAPITAL RATIOS

The Risk-Based Capital Ratios (Tier I and II Capital/Risk-based Assets, and Tier I/Risk-based Assets) are more sensitive to mark-to-market capital adjustments than the Tier I/Total Assets ratio. Table 3.1 illustrates this relationship wherein both Risk-based Capital Ratios declined by 73 basis points (from 10.00 percent to 9.27 percent and 8.57 percent to 7.84 percent) whereas Tier I/Total Assets Ratio declined by only 51 basis points (from 6.00 percent to 5.49 percent) when rates rose 300 basis points. This sensitivity is due to the fact that the Risk-based Capital Ratios have a smaller denominator—risk-based assets are less than total assets—in the ratio calculation. Because of this greater sensitivity, the Risk-based Capital Ratios should have a somewhat larger "cushion" built into them when determining the amount of the "optimum" available-for-sale portfolio.

INVESTMENT CLASSIFICATION RECOMMENDATIONS

The investment classification recommendations described in the notes and comments above are summarized below. Please be sure to review the detailed comments above to be certain that these recommendations apply to your institution.

Available-for-Sale	Held-to-Maturity
Treasuries	**Treasuries**
• Treasuries for liquidity	• Treasuries for pledging
• Treasuries for short-term strategy	• Treasuries for long term strategy
Agencies	**Agencies**
• Putables	• Callables and structured issues (e.g., step-ups, IANs, formula floaters) to avoid capital risk
• Bullets for liquidity	
Tax-exempts	**Tax-exempts**
• Insured AAA tax-exempts for liquidity	• Low- and nonrated exempts
	• TEFRA-advantaged and CRA-type tax-exempts
CMOs	**CMOs**
• Best CMOs for liquidity	• Best sequentials to avoid capital risk (consult with bank examiners
• High-risk or near high-risk to manage closely	

MBS ARMs	MBS ARMs
• Low OAS duration for liquidity	• High OAS duration to avoid capital risk

MBS Fixed Rate	MBS Fixed Rate
• Low duration for liquidity	• High duration to avoid capital risk
• Some "keepers" with gains to start out with capital cushion	

Corporate and Other	Corporate and Other
• Total return securities	• Buy-and-hold securities

GAINS TRADING AND OTHER FINANCIAL MANAGEMENT ISSUES

In the past, the sale of investment securities has occurred for a wide variety of reasons, from harvesting gains to pruning losers, and everything in between. The abuse of "gains trading" was a practice limited to a small minority of institutions, and their actions were apparent from a quick reading of the financial statements.

Statement 115 prevents institutions from selling securities from the held-to-maturity category, except for certain permissible transactions, which exclude about 99 percent of all the reasons for which you would want to sell an investment. There are no limits on the sale of securities from the available-for-sale category. However, institutions should conduct trading activities in the trading account.

Institutions that classify most of the investment portfolio as held-to-maturity should view this action as the "sale" of their option to manage these securities because future penalties (tainting, increased scrutiny of investment documentation and transactions, etc.) for selling held-to-maturity securities far outweigh the benefits of such a transgression. Institutions must evaluate the pros and cons of selling this option and decide whether the compensation received (primarily a prospective reduction of capital volatility) outweighs the opportunity cost (primarily reduced liquidity, inability to manage the portfolio, and the inability to realize gains and losses) of selling the option.

Additional financial management questions to consider include the following:

1. Should the institution adopt Statement 115 by including investment gains in the available-for-sale category

"The abuse of 'gains trading' was a practice limited to a small minority of institutions, and their actions were apparent from a quick reading of the financial statements."

to start out with a positive capital adjustment? What are competitors doing along these lines?

2. Will the institution *ever* want to book investment gains to offset unexpected loan loss provisions or other crisis situations?

3. Does the institution have enough available-for-sale securities to provide ample liquidity?

4. Does the institution have too many available-for-sale securities and related capital risk?

Chapters 2 and 3 have established a methodology to answer these and other questions in a framework to make the investment classification decisions required to successfully manage the investment portfolio under Statement 115.

SUMMARY

After an institution has determined the approximate size of the available-for-sale category, the process of choosing individual securities for this category becomes somewhat easier. The decision of how an institution will manage the available-for-sale category will affect the classification of the investment portfolio. There are two opposing investment management philosophies—total return and buy-and-hold. Chapter 3 describes several methodologies for choosing securities for the available-for-sale category and includes a Mark-to-Market Worksheet and related Classification Notes to help the portfolio manager to evaluate "what-if" scenarios to choose the best securities for the available-for-sale category.

ENDNOTES:

1. Mark-to-Market Worksheet developed by Steve R. Slade, Wachovia Bank of Georgia, N.A., as follow-up to Wachovia Mark-to-Market Investment Conference.

Chapter 4: Managing the Investment Portfolio

Table of Contents—

Is There Life after Mark-to-Market?
Buy-and-Hold Investment Management
Total Return Investment Management
Total Return versus Buy-and-Hold
Interest Rates
  Implied Forward Rates
  Horizon Analysis
Asset/Liability Management
Mutual Funds
Structured Debt Securities
Summary
Types of Structured Debt Securities

Chapter 2 described the process for determining the optimum amount of securities to be held in the available-for-sale category. Chapter 3 described how to choose the best securities for this category. Chapter 4 reviews investment management philosophies and related topics to be considered in managing the investment portfolio in a mark-to-market era.

IS THERE LIFE AFTER MARK-TO-MARKET?

The implementation of Statement 115 will be a difficult period of time for the management of the investment portfolio. Bank examiners and independent accountants are expected to take an active role in reviewing the implementation of Statement 115. Bank regulatory agencies are in the process of issuing guidelines for the adoption of Statement 115. Independent accounting firms, which have responsibility for financial statement compliance with Statement 115, will review an institution's documentation and classification decisions.

The advice, counsel and approval of bank examiners and independent accountants is important to the successful adoption of Statement 115. Institutions should document the planning and implementation of Statement 115 so that bank examiners and independent accountants can easily follow investment assumptions and goals. Institutions that are ill-prepared to implement Statement 115 will have a more difficult time defending their plans for managing the investment portfolio.

In particular, institutions should expect to face resistance towards classifying certain securities (e.g., CMOs, MBS, structured debt securities) in the held-to-maturity category. As discussed further in Chapter 6, bank examiners have commented, "Prudent bank managers cannot and should not disregard the effects of changes in market factors on those securities that they intend to hold to maturity."[1] By including such securities in the held-to-maturity category, institutions must necessarily "disregard" market factors because securities can be sold only under rare circumstances. However, as discussed in Chapter 3, such securities are better suited for the held-to-maturity category because they have too much price volatility and too little liquidity.

Institutions must remember that they have the burden of proof to justify assumptions and document the classification of investments with sound logic and a track record of compliance. Differences of opinion on how to classify securities are bound to occur; Statement 115 is too subjective to think otherwise. Also, institutions must bear in mind that the initial implementation of Statement 115 may be the easy part. Institutions will probably get the benefit of the doubt if there are any close calls on classifying investments under the innocent until proven guilty theory. However, infractions will not be treated so kindly.

Most institutions will adopt Statement 115 with a mark-to-market gain in the available-for-sale category. This is a "good news/bad news" situation. The good news is that there should be an increase to shareholders' equity at the date of adoption (December 31, 1993 or January 1, 1994). While this additional capital dilutes capital ratios as discussed in Chapter 2, it provides a cushion to buffer the available-for-sale category against rising interest rates. The bad news is that the mark-to-market gain (or loss) will decline to zero as the securities are held to maturity. Even if rates stay the same, the Unrealized Gain or Loss Equity Account (Chapter 6, Accounting and Financial Reporting) will decrease as the securities in this category mature. If the institution follows a passive buy-and-hold investment management style in the available-for-sale category, capital erosion *will* occur because the securities will mature to cash.

> *"Most institutions will adopt Statement 115 with a mark-to-market gain in the available-for-sale category."*

Institutions may be able to mitigate this erosion and enhance returns of the investment portfolio by exploring a more *active* investment management style. Both the active and passive investment management styles are summarized below.

BUY-AND-HOLD INVESTMENT MANAGEMENT

Buy-and-hold investment management, sometimes referred to in fixed income research and texts as "passive" investment management, has been the predominant strategy used by financial institutions to manage the investment portfolio. This strategy will be used exclusively for the held-to-maturity investment category. In addition, many institutions will use this strategy to manage investments classified in the available-for-sale category.

Buy-and-hold investment management is a strategy of holding a properly structured investment portfolio to maturity without attempting to "outperform" other investors by finding "cheap" securities or trading the portfolio. Buy-and-hold investors are most concerned about choosing the best security to enhance the interest rate margin or spread of the institution. Analysis is focused on finding a security that will complement the institution's other banking activities.

An important thought about the buy-and-hold investment philosophy is that investment securities with maturities of more than five years (core investments) represent approximately 35 percent of total investment securities for the average institution.[2] If an institution has an investment portfolio that is 20 percent of total assets, then core investments would represent 7 percent (one-fifth of 35) of total assets, which is the approximate capitalization ratio of an institution. This is probably more of a mathematical coincidence than anything else but it is an interesting relationship for institutions to ponder as they seek guidance in determining the amount of held-to-maturity investments.

TOTAL RETURN INVESTMENT MANAGEMENT

Total rate of return investment management, sometimes referred to in fixed income research and texts as "active" investment management, has been the predominant strategy used by mutual funds and common trust funds to manage investments. Total return investment managers believe they can out-perform buy-and-hold investors through superior market forecasting and superior ability to find cheap securities through analytics and trading the portfolio. In adopting Statement 115, some institutions will move closer to a total return philosophy to manage available-for-sale investments.

Total return is measured by dividing net interest income *and* mark-to-market gains and losses by the market value of investments. Institutions should begin measuring and analyzing the total return of available-for-sale investments, even if total return strategies are not followed. The total rate of return can be calculated using average balance information included in the annual report. Thus, bank analysts and competitors will know the performance of each institution's available-for-sale portfolio.

Broadly speaking, there are two sources of potential value in active bond management. The first is interest rate forecasting, which tries to anticipate changes in the direction of interest rates, spread relationships, or the slope of the yield curve.

Yield curve theory suggests that, in an efficient market, the market's collective wisdom about the future has been reflected, or discounted, in current interest rates. This brings to mind a telling joke about two economists walking down the street. They spot a $20 bill on the sidewalk. One economist (a total return investor) starts to pick it up, but the other economist (a buy-and-hold investor) says, "Don't bother, if the bill were real, someone would have picked it up already." Along these lines, total return investors do not necessarily assume that interest rates are "fairly" set, for the market in general or for a specific security.

Total return investors attempt to anticipate changes in interest rates. If declines are anticipated, investors should increase portfolio duration, and vice versa. It should be noted that these techniques will generate exceptional returns only if the investor's information or insight is superior to that of the market. It is somewhat difficult to profit from knowledge that rates are about to fall if everyone else in the market is aware of this. Anticipated lower future interest rates are already built into bond prices in the sense that long-term bonds are already selling at higher prices. If the institution does not have information or insights before the market does, it will be too late to act on that information if prices will have responded already to the news.

The second source of potential profit is employing some form of technical analysis to identify specific securities or sectors that are cheap to the market. Swap ideas are generated based upon the ability to buy and sell investments without regard to original cost, which increases the opportunity to improve returns. Of course, while an investment swap may be advantageous on its own merit, institutions cannot completely disregard historical cost accounting because of related income statement and capital planning considerations involved in the sale of securities.

Institutions must periodically conduct buy/hold/sell evaluations to determine if the reason a security was initially purchased is still valid. For example, institutions can simulate performance of the current investment portfolio in different rate environments (e.g., rising, falling, and flat) to determine price volatility (duration), income return, and cash flow variability under changing prepayments. If conditions have changed such that the institution would no longer purchase a particular security, then a swap or other investment action may be warranted.

In planning total return strategies, the portfolio manager must be certain that investments have adequate liquidity (low bid/ask spread). Also, a more active portfolio management style requires a working knowledge of the investment markets. Institutions without this knowledge or experience should retain the counsel of a competent portfolio advisor. Otherwise, institutions would be better off to follow a buy-and-hold strategy and to emphasize investment yield over liquidity when selecting investments.

Total return strategies and considerations include the following:

- Sell what is rich and buy what is cheap.
- Follow option-adjusted spread as a performance benchmark.
- Maintain high liquidity in portfolio.
- Follow mark-to-market accounting.
- Turn portfolio one to two times per year.
- Attempt to stay even with the market and catch one or two bond rallies per year.
- Use duration concepts (shorten during rising rates, lengthen during falling rates.)
- Use stop-loss limits.
- Use static and dynamic hedging products.

"In planning total return strategies, the portfolio manager must be certain that investments have adequate liquidity (low bid/ask spread)."

TOTAL RETURN VERSUS BUY-AND-HOLD

Advocates of both the total return and buy-and-hold investment management philosophies have their own arguments as to why their strategies are superior.

Proponents of the buy-and-hold investment management philosophy believe that the efficient market hypothesis renders active portfolio management as largely a wasted effort, unlikely to justify the additional expense required to support the additional analyses. Therefore, they advocate more of a passive investment strategy that makes no attempt to outsmart the market. A passive strategy aims only at structuring a well-diversified portfolio of securities without attempting to trade the portfolio.

Proponents of the total return investment management philosophy believe that their strategies can add 50 to 100 basis points to the performance of investments. Advocates of the total return philosophy point out that buy-and-hold investors have become complacent from the strong bull market of the past decade and that if rates begin to rise, more aggressive strategies will be required. In addition, the ongoing deregulation and increased competition for customer deposits (e.g., mutual funds) and other factors have created an upheaval in historical spread relationships. These changes warrant not only a more active investment management philosophy, but also a more aggressive management of the liability side as well.

INTEREST RATES

Yield curve theory (i.e., expectations hypothesis) suggests that the shape of the yield curve sends us a message about the future direction of interest rates—especially when the curve is either unusually positive or unusually negative (such as the early 1980s).

Implied Forward Rates

The theory of *implied forward rates* suggests that future interest rates can be calculated mathematically based on the current yield curve. Yield curve theory suggests that, in an efficient market, the market's collective wisdom about the future has been reflected, or discounted, in current interest rates. Therefore, in theory, an investor is indifferent about choosing between what are really equal investment scenarios.

For example, using Table 4.1, Implied Forward U.S. Treasury Yields derived from the Bloomberg System, an investor would be indifferent between the following two investment choices: 1) invest in a three year security at a yield of 4.10 percent or, 2) invest in a two-year security at 3.82 percent followed by a one-year security in two years at the implied forward rate of 4.68 percent for an average yield of 4.10 percent—(3.82 percent + 3.82 percent + 4.68 percent)/3 = 4.10 percent. Both investments have a yield of 4.10 percent and the investor, with a leap of faith, is indifferent between the two choices.

Implied forward yield curve theory is, at market extremes, a fairly good predictor of the future direction of interest rates.

Table 4.1 Implied Forward U.S. Treasury Yields

Years to Maturity

Year	1	2	3	4	5	7	10	20	30
Today	3.32	3.82	4.10	4.40	4.69	4.88	5.32	5.65	5.99
Forward									
1		4.31	4.50	4.76	5.03	5.08	5.27	5.57	5.81
2		4.68	4.98	5.27	5.27	5.30	5.56	5.74	5.91
3		5.28	5.57	5.47	5.46	5.58	5.84	5.88	6.00
5		5.26	5.35	5.58	5.77	5.95	5.94	6.00	6.10

However, the amplitude and timing of such interest rate forecasts is not considered to be very reliable.

Figure 4.1 is a graphic display of the current, one-year and five-year forward yield curves.

Horizon Analysis

One form of interest rate forecasting is called *horizon analysis* whereby an investor selects a particular holding period and

Figure 4.1 Implied Forward Yield Curves

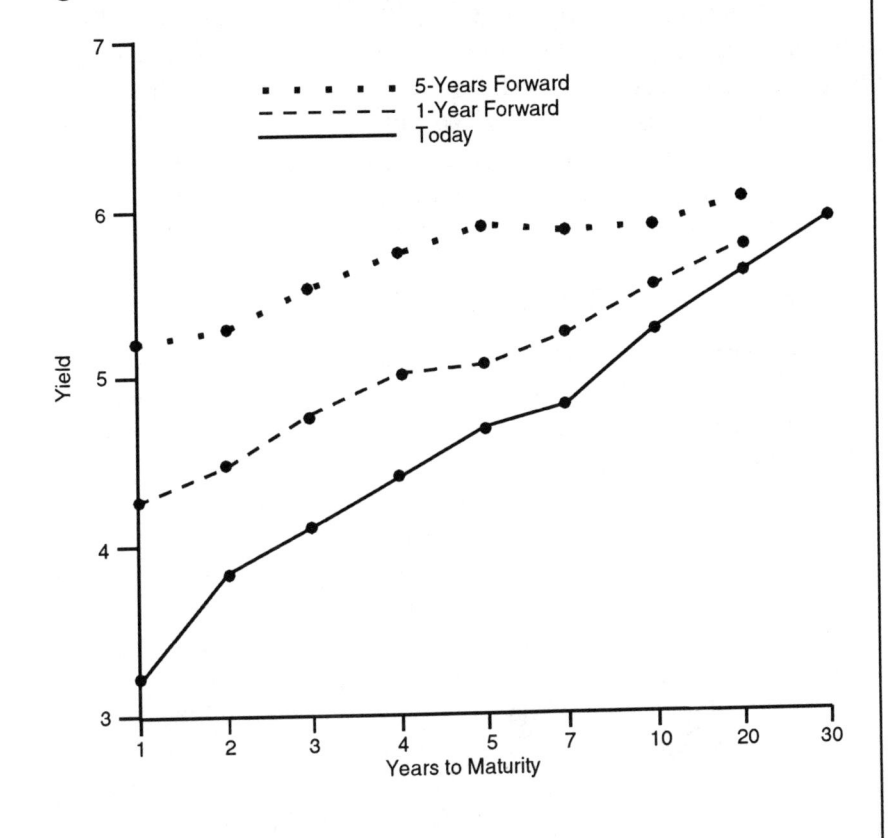

predicts the yield curve at the end of that period. Based on the predicted yield curve at the end of the holding period, the investor can ascertain the market value of the security. The investor's total return would be the coupon income and the prospective investment gain.

For example, an investor may choose an FNMA teaser ARM with an initial coupon of 3.75 percent, a 9.75 percent lifetime cap, and a 2.30 percent margin tied to the one year constant maturity treasury (CMT), which is currently at 3.30 percent. The investor intends to hold this bond for one year and predicts that the yield curve will be unchanged from today. Therefore, the coupon will reset to 5.60 percent and the market value of the ARM will increase by one point to a level where fully indexed ARMs are currently priced. The total return for the holding period would be 3.75 percent plus the one point investment gain. This 4.75 percent total return exceeds the current yield on fully indexed ARMs by an estimated 15 basis points.

A particular version of horizon analysis is called *riding the yield curve*. If the yield curve is upward sloping and if it is projected that the curve will not shift during the investment horizon, then the security will "ride" the yield curve toward the lower yields of a shorter-term security. The decrease in yield will result in an investment gain on the security, which will contribute to a higher total return. The danger of riding the yield curve is that the yield curve will never stay the same forever and at some point it will shift upward. Indeed, according to yield curve theory, an upward sloping curve is evidence that market participants expect interest rates to be rising over time.

ASSET/LIABILITY MANAGEMENT

Statement 115 increases the opportunities for institutions to use asset/liability (A/L) management to manage interest rate risk. In the past, opportunities to sell securities were limited because of portfolio accounting restrictions. Now the interest rate risk of the institution can be managed more readily by modifying the duration of the available-for-sale category. Strategies to improve the margin and reduce interest rate risk can be generated through the asset/liability management process.

Institutions have developed sophisticated asset/liability (A/L) management models to measure the interest rate sensitivity of their balance sheets. Institutions should bear in mind that the A/L management process may become even more important now that regulatory officials are on the verge of finalizing interest rate risk proposals. Some of these A/L models calculate static gap, the difference between the amount of rate-sensitive assets, and rate-sensitive liabilities.

One way to view gap management is that an institution is attempting to equate the duration of assets and liabilities to effectively *immunize* the institution's overall exposure to changes in interest rates. If the duration of assets and liabilities is equal, changes in interest rates would have a net change effect of zero.

Gap management can be used strategically to help an institution increase net income based on its interest rate outlook. For example, if an institution expects short-term interest rates to increase in the near term, it might position the balance sheet to be asset-sensitive (i.e., a positive gap with interest-sensitive assets exceeding interest-sensitive liabilities). Therefore, if interest rates rise, net interest income would increase. An institution expecting interest rates to fall in the near term might position the balance sheet to be liability sensitive (i.e., a negative gap with interest sensitive liabilities exceeding interest-sensitive assets). Therefore, if interest rates fall, net interest income would increase.

Simulation-based models are forward looking, requiring assumptions about changes in loan demand, deposit growth, and the yield curve, as well as managerial behavior. Simulation models can be used to calculate changes in the institution's net interest margin under different interest rate scenarios (e.g., up and down 200 basis points). This analysis can be used to help an institution determine the extent that the investment portfolio will be used to manage the interest sensitivity of the institution.

Financial institutions are able to reduce interest rate risk not only through investment products, but also through the creative development of new banking products—both fixed and variable rate. Products such as ARMs, home equity loans, floating rate credit card loans, NOW accounts, and MMDAs are examples of creative solutions to banking problems in the past. However, as the financial services industry becomes more competitive, opportunities to resolve gap and interest sensitivity problems may diminish. For example, in the late 1980s and 1990s, consumers have accelerated their withdrawals of bank deposits and have invested these funds outside of the banking system in mutual funds. Institutions must be nimble and learn to solve interest rate risk problems through new solutions. Institutions cannot rely on past solutions to solve future problems.

MUTUAL FUNDS

The advent of mark-to-market investment accounting has stirred new interest by financial institutions in the purchase of mutual

"Simulation-based models are forward looking, requiring assumptions about changes in loan demand, deposit growth, and the yield curve, as well as managerial behavior."

funds for the investment portfolio. Mutual funds are "marketable equity securities" and therefore must be included in the Trading Account or Available-for-Sale categories, depending on the purpose of the investment.

Some institutions have evaluated a novel investment plan whereby discrete securities would be purchased for the held-to-maturity category and mutual funds would be purchased for the available-for-sale category. The mutual funds would be purchased in lieu of short-term investments to satisfy liquidity needs.

Part of the appeal of mutual funds is that an institution has instant access to professional portfolio management and the latest in hardware and software, without having to buy it themselves. Of course, mutual funds charge a management fee or some sort of sales charge, so this expertise is not free. Mutual funds are particularly attractive to smaller institutions that do not have investment expertise in-house. Another advantage of mutual funds is that gains and losses in securities within the fund are reflected in net asset value and would not be reflected on the income statement until the mutual fund is sold.

The biggest disadvantage of investments in mutual funds is that these securities are capital assets for tax purposes and losses must be offset against capital gains. If an institution has no capital gains, then the loss on mutual funds is not deductible on the tax return. This tax loss issue is significant because the law of averages suggests that mutual funds will have capital losses at some point in the future. Some investors that purchased mutual funds in 1986 and 1987, when interest rates were low, are still waiting to sell their mutual fund investments at a profit.

STRUCTURED DEBT SECURITIES

One of the interesting developments of the 1990s has been the financial engineering of securities issued by the U.S. government agencies. The U.S. government continues to issue Treasury securities but the agencies have revamped their debt issuance programs to include a wide variety of structured debt securities.

Figures 4.2 and 4.3 illustrate how the Federal Home Loan Bank System (FHLB) has revamped the issuance of their debt securities. Other agencies such as the Federal National Mortgage Association (FNMA), Federal Home Loan Mortgage Corporation (FHLMC), and Tennessee Valley Authority (TVA) are also issuing structured debt securities. The amount of fixed rate, fixed term

Figure 4.2 FHLB Bonds Sold

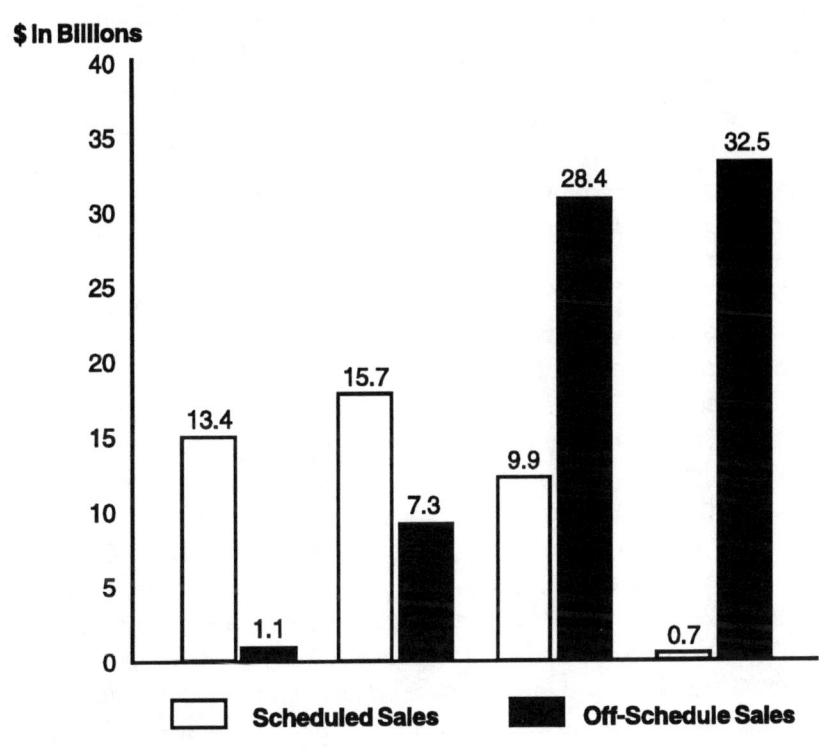

$ In Billions

- 13.4 / 1.1
- 15.7 / 7.3
- 9.9 / 28.4
- 0.7 / 32.5

☐ Scheduled Sales ■ Off-Schedule Sales

* Through 8/31/93

Figure 4.3 FHLB Consolidated Bonds Issued ($ in billions) Year-to-Date 1993

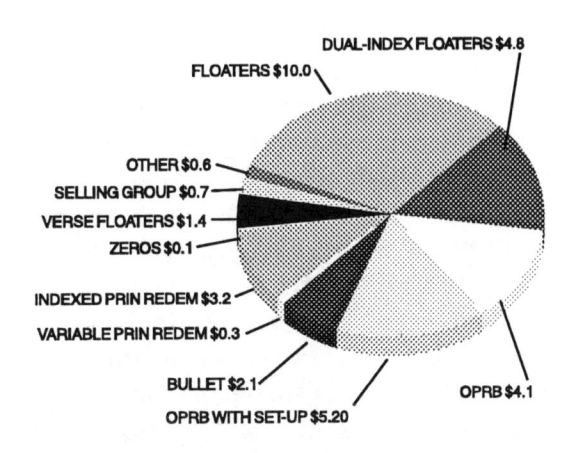

- DUAL-INDEX FLOATERS $4.8
- FLOATERS $10.0
- OTHER $0.6
- SELLING GROUP $0.7
- VERSE FLOATERS $1.4
- ZEROS $0.1
- INDEXED PRIN REDEM $3.2
- VARIABLE PRIN REDEM $0.3
- BULLET $2.1
- OPRB WITH SET-UP $5.20
- OPRB $4.1

* Through 8/31/93

Managing the Investment Portfolio 59

("bullet") securities accounted for less than 10 percent of securities issued during 1993 by the FHLB. Floaters and dual indexed floaters accounted for nearly 50 percent of bonds issued by the FHLB. A partial listing of over 50 different structured debt securities issued by the FHLB in 1993 is included in Appendix A.

The significance of these structured debt securities for financial institutions is twofold. First, as investors, institutions should understand the structure of the investments they are buying. These structured debt securities include features to benefit the issuer, not the investor. Institutions should take the initiative to determine the type of security needed for its own purposes. If an institution needs a five year, fixed rate security, it should buy a U.S. Treasury, not a five year callable step-up that may be gone in two years.

The second message for institutions to ponder is the extent that structured debt and derivative securities have reached in today's financial marketplace. Certainly the FHLB has more opportunities to engineer structured transactions than the average financial institution. However, financial institutions should gear up to understand the pros and cons of financial engineering and be alert to opportunities to use such concepts to manage interest rate risk and enhance the net interest margin. Chapter 5, Hedging the Portfolio with Derivatives, discusses uses of derivative for financial institutions.

SUMMARY

The implementation of Statement 115 will be a difficult period of time for the management of the investment portfolio. Institutions that are ill-prepared to implement Statement 115 will have a more difficult time defending their plans for managing the investment portfolio. Institutions must remember that they have the burden of proof to justify assumptions and document the classification of investments with sound logic and a track record of compliance. Most institutions will adopt Statement 115 with a mark-to-market gain, which is a "good news/bad news" situation. Some institutions will use a buy-and-hold investment management philosophy, which is a strategy of holding a properly structured investment portfolio to maturity without attempting to "outperform" other investors by finding "cheap" securities or trading the portfolio. Other institutions will use a total return investment management philosophy, believing they can out-perform buy-and-hold investors through superior market forecasting or superior ability to find cheap securities through analytics and trading the portfolio. Yield curve theory suggests that the shape of the yield curve sends us a message about the future direction of interest rates. Implied forward rates and horizon analysis are used by investors to develop strategies to enhance total return. Statement 115 increases the opportunities for institutions to use asset/liability management to manage interest rate risk. Financial institutions are able to reduce interest rate risk not only through investment products, but also through the creative development of new banking products. The advent of mark-to-market investment accounting has stirred new interest by financial institutions in the purchase of mutual funds and structured debt securities.

TYPES OF STRUCTURED DEBT SECURITIES

Following is a partial list of securities issued by the FHLB during 1993. The brief description of these securities shown below gives some indication as to the magnitude and complexity of structured debt securities used in the financial marketplace today.

- Constant Maturity Treasury (CMT) Floater.
- Stepped CMT Floater.
- Floored CMT Floater.
- Collared CMT Floater.
- Stepped Floored CMT Floater
- LIBOR (London Interbank Offered Rate) Floater.
- Collared LIBOR Floater.
- Floored LIBOR Floater.
- LIBOR Optional Principal Redemption (i.e., partially callable) Bonds (OPBR) Floater.
- Stepped Inverse LIBOR Floater.
- Inverse LIBOR Floater.
- Inverse Floored LIBOR Floater.
- Prime Floater.
- Floored Prime Floater.
- Stepped Floored T-Bill Floater.
- Collared T-Bill Floater
- Capped T-Bill Floater.
- T-Bill Floater.
- Inverse Fed Funds Floater.

- Fed Funds Floater Inverse Principal Redemption Bond (IPRB).
- Cost of Funds Index (COFI) Floater.
- COFI Floater OPRB.
- Inverse Swedish Krona (SKR) (STIBOR) Floater.
- Inverse French Franc (FFR) Swap Rate Floater.
- OPRB—3 Year/1 Year, 5/1, 5/2, 7/1, 7/3.
- Step-up 5 Year/2 Year OPRB.
- Bullets (1.5 Year, 2 Year, 3 Year, 4 1/3 Year and 5 Year).
- Inverse Italian (ITL) Swap Rate Floater.
- Inverse Deutsche Mark (DM) LIBOR Floater.
- Floored Inverse DM LIBOR Floater.
- Public Securities Association (PSA) Index Floater.
- Dual Index Floater.
- Floored Dual Index Floater.
- Noncallable Multi Step-Up.
- Inverse Principal Redemption Bond (IPRB)-LIBOR.
- IPRB-PSA.
- IPRB-LIBOR.
- Scheduled Principal Redemption Bond.
- Scheduled/Indexed Principal Redemption Bond.
- Variable Principal Redemption Bond.
- Variable Principal Redemption LIBOR Floater.
- Inverse ITL LIBOR Floater.
- Inverse Deutsche Mark (DM) Swap Rate Floater.
- Inverse European Currency Unit (ECU) Swap Rate Floater.
- Inverse Spanish Peseta LIBOR Floater.
- Inverse French Franc (FFR) PIBOR Floater.
- Multi-indexed Floater.
- Floored Dual Index Floater.
- Canadian Swap Rate Floater.

- LIBOR Floater IPRB.
- Stepped Dual Index Floater.
- Capped LIBOR Floater.
- IPRB (Scored)—PSA.
- T-Bill Floater OPRB.
- Dual Indexed OPRB Floater.
- Capped Lira LIBOR Floater.
- Capped S & P 500 Floater.
- Floored Dual-indexed OPRB Floater.
- Inverse LIBOR OPRB Floater.
- Inverse LIBOR IPRB.

ENDNOTES

1. Comment letter from Comptroller of the Currency, Administrator of National Banks, to the Financial Accounting Standards Board, January 12, 1993, p.1.

2. *Bank Performance Digest,* IDC Finanical Publishing, Inc., as of March 31, 1993

Chapter 5:
Hedging the Portfolio with Derivatives

Table of Contents—

Regulatory Concerns about Derivatives
Convexity
Interest Rate Swaps
  Credit Risk
  Types of Swaps
Forwards
  Forward Contract
Forward Rate Agreement
Interest Rate Caps
Interest Rate Floors
Interest Rate Collars
Futures Contracts
Options
  Option Buyer
  Option Seller
Interest Rate Volatility and the Investment Portfolio
Hedging the Investment Portfolio
  Hedge Strategies
  Accounting for Hedges—GAAP
  Accounting for Hedges—Tax
Derivative Analytics and Operating Systems
Summary
Suggestions for Further Reading

Derivative instruments are financial contracts that derive their value from another asset, interest rate, exchange rate, or index. This is a relatively broad definition and would include some instruments such as mortgage-backed securities and collateralized mortgage obligations. A more limited definition would include interest rate and cross-currency swaps; commodity swaps; caps, floors, and collars; forwards, futures, and options; and similar agreements or options to enter into any of the above. Depending upon what is included in the definition of derivatives, estimates for the notional amount of the global derivatives market range from $7 trillion to $15.5 trillion.

U.S. banks are major players in the derivative markets. However, approximately 99 percent of the derivative activities conducted by U.S. commercial banks take place in banking companies with more than $10 billion in assets.[1] In recent years, regional banks have become active in these markets. According to the findings of an Ernst & Young survey[2], financial institutions are expected to increase hedging activity to reduce earnings or price volatility and related capital risk in response to Statement 115.

The purpose of this chapter is twofold: 1) to identify the primary derivative instruments that can be used to hedge the market value of the investment portfolio and 2) to identify the significant management issues and strategies that should be evaluated by institutions involved in derivatives. Institutions contemplating the use of derivative products must conduct thorough research that goes beyond the scope of material included in this chapter. A bibliography of suggestions for further readings on derivative products and investment strategies is included at the end of this chapter.

REGULATORY CONCERNS ABOUT DERIVATIVES

Because of regulatory and other concerns about financial and operational risk, institutions have more stringent requirements for documenting policies, procedures, and internal controls for derivative instruments. In December 1992, the Comptroller of the Currency issued *An Examiner's Guide to Investment Products and Practices*[3], which has extensive coverage of derivative products, including guidance on risk-based capital ratios, legal limitations, accounting treatment, and intrinsic and operational risks. Pages 81 through 98 of this guide written on derivative products are reprinted in Appendix A for references purposes.

In a September 1993 speech[4], the Comptroller of the Currency called for the creation of an interagency task force to address the involvement of U.S. banks in derivative products. In this same speech, the Comptroller commented:

> The OCC must ensure that national banks engaging in derivatives transactions, either as dealers or as end-users, have the ability to accurately assess the risks associated with financial derivatives activities and have

sound risk management systems. In this way, banks can be expected to protect themselves against large losses resulting from counterparty failures or from adverse movements in market rates.

The interagency task force is concerned not only with derivative activities conducted by corporate finance departments of financial institutions, but also with derivative instruments used to manage the institution's overall interest rate risk.

The *American Banker*[5] recently reported that Banc One Corp., an institution with a balance sheet of $75 billion, has $31 billion notional value of interest rate swaps recorded on the *other balance sheet*—the "derivatives balance sheet." Banc One was asset sensitive and was concerned about the effects of falling interest rates. In the past, this asset sensitivity would have been remedied by purchasing fixed rate investments, funded with short term, floating rate liabilities. But Banc One thought that buying securities would strain capital ratios and the assortment of securities available in the market was not acceptable. Approximately one-third of these swaps are forward swaps, or contracts whose performance will commence in future periods. In the case of Banc One, interest rate swaps (excluding other derivatives products such as options and futures) is 41 percent of the total of traditional assets and liabilities captured on the statement of financial condition.

Salomon Brothers, Inc. reported[6] that during the two years ending December 31, 1992, that the nation's 150 largest banking companies increased the face value of their options portfolio by $400 billion to more than $1 trillion and increased their portfolios of futures and forward contracts by approximately $1 trillion to $1.75 trillion.

What are financial institutions attempting to do? Beyond the advantageous regulatory and accounting rules, financial institutions are attempting to manage *convexity*.

CONVEXITY

Portfolio managers are increasingly learning to measure the convexity of a security (or derivative instrument) and attempt to buy and sell convexity like a commodity. Understanding and valuing convexity is important for managing the investment portfolio, because in many cases the duration measure (see Chapter 3) alone is inadequate for predicting a security's expected return performance. The duration and convexity measures, used together, provide a more accurate prediction of performance.

> "The interagency task force is concerned not only with derivative activities conducted by corporate finance departments of financial institutions, but also with derivative instruments used to manage the institution's overall interest rate risk."

A review of definitions of duration and convexity would help illustrate the relationship between these two investment terms.

- *Duration or Macaulay Duration* is the weighted average term to maturity, is also a measure of the price sensitivity of a bond for a particular change in interest rates.

- *Modified or Effective Duration* refines Macaulay duration somewhat and is defined as the percent change in the price of a bond for a small change in interest rates. This measure does not consider any embedded options, such as scheduled calls or mortgage prepayments.

- *OAS (Option Adjusted Spread) Duration* refines modified duration to consider any embedded options in a bond, such as puts and calls.

- *Convexity* is the change in duration as yields change. Using an analogy, if duration is speed, then convexity would be acceleration. When large shifts in interest rates occur, bonds with positive convexity perform better than bonds with negative convexity.

- *OAS (Option Adjusted Spread) Convexity* measures the change of duration as yields change considering any embedded options in a bond, such as puts and call.

Defined mathematically, convexity measures the extent to which the price/yield curve is nonlinear. To the portfolio manager, positive convexity is considered good because the price of a security with positive convexity (e.g., U.S. Treasury security) goes up more in a bull market than it goes down in a bear market. On the other hand, negative convexity is considered bad because the price of a security with negative convexity (e.g., mortgage-backed securities) goes down more in a bear market that it goes up in a bull market.

During the bull market of the last several years, portfolio managers with mortgage-backed securities found how vexing this property of negative convexity can be. Tremendous opportunity gains were lost by some institutions because of excessive positions in mortgage securities. But having negative convexity in a bull market is not nearly as harmful as having negative convexity in a bear market. Of course, the optimum position is positive convexity in a bull market.

Managing convexity is more complex than just increasing or decreasing the levels of this measure. Derivative traders deal with convexity like a commodity, performing relative-value analysis of different deal structures and simulating price performance under different interest rate scenarios. The goal is to buy (increase) convexity when it is cheap and sell (decrease) convexity when it is rich. This rich/cheap analysis depends heavily on projections of interest rate volatility and changes in interest rates. In a stable rate environment, for example, selling convexity provides yield enhancements compared to a neutral convexity position. The risk, of course, is that interest rates increase with negative convexity accelerating the decline of investment value.

Unlike traditional investment products, where increasing positive convexity is difficult to achieve, increasing positive convexity is quite easy with the assortment of derivative instruments available today. These instruments are discussed more fully in the remainder of this chapter. However, the following example will quickly illustrate the power of a derivative instrument.

For example, buying a call option (i.e., the right to buy a bond) provides an investor with positive convexity because the option provides limited downside protection (i.e., the cost of the option) if rates increase and substantial upside returns if rates decrease. However, when an instrument incorporates a short call position (e.g., a callable bond where the investor has the obligation to "sell" a security at the call price), the outcome is reversed. If interest rates decrease, the upside return is limited because the bond will be called, and the loss can be substantial when interest rates increase. Similar to buying a call option, buying a put option (i.e., the right to sell a security) also provides an investor with positive convexity because the option provides limited downside protection (i.e., the cost of the option) if rates decrease and unlimited upside returns if rates increase.

INTEREST RATE SWAPS

Swaps are private agreements between two counterparties to exchange cash flows in the future according to a prearranged formula.

By way of background, interest rate swaps originated in 1981 primarily to provide businesses with a tool to change floating rate obligations into fixed rate obligations, and vice versa. Banks became involved in swap agreements because banks commonly have advantages in making credit decisions, finding counterparties, and acting as intermediaries between two borrowers with offsetting financial needs. Swaps were another variation on traditional banking services.

But banks could not always find both counterparties necessary to construct a matched position. As a consequence, banks began to write swaps with only one counterparty at a time, and then try to generate a synthetic match to that position with other

> *"Credit risk, or performance risk, is the risk that a counterparty fails to perform as contractually bound."*

types of financial instruments (e.g., U.S. government securities) until a matching swap could be located. Banks began to "warehouse" swaps, and the swap market began to grow rapidly.

The market also began to grow in new directions. Sophisticated, more complex products were introduced, primarily to meet the individual financial needs of bank customers. Derivatives became highly successful risk management tools. Along these lines, banks found that these innovative financial instruments provided low-cost funding alternatives with greater flexibility in managing their own interest rate risk.

Credit Risk

Credit risk, or performance risk, is the risk that a counterparty fails to perform as contractually bound. The credit risk loss exposure is equal to the cost of replacing the swap when it has positive value. If the counterparty defaults when the swap has negative value, there is no loss to the institution.

Credit risk is an immediate risk incurred at the inception of the swap. Because most swaps have zero initial cost, credit risk is initially deemed to be zero. However, if rates increase dramatically after the swap is executed, then the swap will increase in market value and, accordingly, credit risk. However, as the swap approaches maturity, credit risk declines to zero.

There are numerous other factors influencing credit risk, including the following[7]:

- *Overall Level of Rates*—Interest rates tend to be more volatile when they are high. Thus, higher interest rates result in higher volatility, which results in greater default exposure.

- *Collateral*—If collateral is pledged, then the risk of default is significantly reduced since possession of collateral would occur in a default situation.

- *Payment Frequency (annual, quarterly, monthly)*—The more frequent swap rates are reset and swap payments occur, the sooner defaults are discovered and remedies can be taken.

- *Fixed Versus Floating*—The credit risk of a pay floating swap is higher because the potential burden of higher cash flows creates higher credit risk in the future. This is particularly true when interest rates are low.

- *Time to Maturity*—Longer maturity swaps have a longer time period during which default could occur and thus have higher credit risk.

- *Volatility of Interest Rates*—The greater the volatility of interest rates, the more likely the counterparty will face large payments with increased credit risk.

In measuring the amount of credit risk, or performance risk, associated with a swap, institutions should consider both the term of the swap and the potential annual loss exposure due to nonperformance. For example, an institution may assess the credit risk on a three year, $1 million swap as $60,000 or 6 percent of notional value calculated as follows: three-year maturity times 2% assumed annual loss equals 6% times $1 million, or $60,000. The assumed annual loss of 2% in this example is estimated based on an *unfavorable* 2 percent change in interest rates. Historically, a 1 to 2 percent change in interest rates is conservative, but a higher or lower loss assumption could be used. In any event, institutions should conduct a credit review of counterparties as if they were making a loan to the counterparty.

When negotiating an interest rate swap, an institution should obtain price quotes from several counterparties, comparing swap price and other terms with counterparty credit risk and service capabilities. Institutions should not necessarily choose the counterparty with the lowest swap price, keeping in mind that counterparties with better credit ratings are able to charge a slightly higher swap price. Similarly, institutions should be aware that their own credit rating will influence the cost of an interest rate swap because performance risk is a two-way street.

Types of Swaps

There are several different types of interest rate swaps, which can be used to achieve different strategies, including the following[8]:

- *Amortizing/Accreting*—The notional principal is changed over the life of the swap, which can be matched against investment and loan cash flows.

- *Basis*—This swap is between two floating interest rates. The need for a basis swap arises when assets and liabilities are both floating, but the floating rate is pegged to different interest rates, such as Treasury bills and Eurodollars.

- *Deferred (forward)*—The swap does not begin until a later date. This type of swap is useful when simulation models suggest interest rate protection is needed in future periods.

- *Circus*—The swap involves currencies as well as interest rates. This type of swap is useful when managing both

> *"During the mid-1980s, many institutions used interest rate swaps to lock-in fixed rate funding for the purchase of mortgage-backed securities."*

currency risk and interest rate risk simultaneously. This swap may be most appropriate for multinational institutions.

- *Extendable*—One counterparty has the right to lengthen the swap. This option feature adds flexibility to the swap holder, allowing the holder to extend the life of the swap if interest sensitivity imbalances persist.

- *Putable*—One counterparty has the right to shorten the swap. This option feature provides the swap holder the ability to unwind the swap if interest rate sensitivity imbalances cease to be a problem.

- *Step-up*—The notional principal is increased over the swap. This unusual variation would be applicable to a financial institution with an increasing gap problem for longer maturities.

- *Swaption*—An option to enter a swap. This is one of the more popular variations of swaps. A swaption is really an option-based product, which allows the swap holder the right to activate the swap if predetermined levels are triggered.

During the mid-1980s, many institutions used interest rate swaps to lock-in fixed rate funding for the purchase of mortgage-backed securities. Institutions anticipated that substantial prepayments would occur if interest rates declined, so swaps were amortized to mirror expected prepayments. However, many of these "first generation" swaps backfired because prepayments were much greater than anticipated. These extraordinary prepayments exposed a costly term funding mismatch. Thus, institutions should remember that interest rate swaps can be used to hedge interest rate risk, but they cannot solve funding risk problems. Many of the swaps described above are "second generation" swaps, which improve upon the "plain vanilla" swaps of the 1980s.

FORWARDS

A *forward rate agreement* is like a one-period interest rate swap where the fixed rate is set at the signing date and the floating rate is set at a specified forward date called the reset date. Integral to understanding a forward rate agreement is the forward contract.

Forward Contract

A *forward contract* is an agreement to buy or sell an asset at a specified future time for a specified price. A forward contract is obligatory to both the buyer and the seller. The contract is usually written by a financial institution and is not normally traded on an exchange. One of the parties to a forward contract assumes a *long position* and agrees to buy the underlying asset on a specified date at a specified price. The other party assumes a *short position* and agrees to sell the asset on the same date for the same price. The specified price in a forward contract is referred to as the *delivery price*. At the signing date when the contract is entered into, the delivery price is chosen so that the value of the forward contract to both parties is zero.[9] This means that there is no initial cost to take either a long or a short position. Accordingly, no cash flows are normally exchanged on the signing date.

A forward contract is normally settled at maturity. The holder of the short position delivers the asset to the holder of the long position in return for a cash amount equal to the delivery price. A key variable determining the value of a forward contract is the market price of the asset. As noted above, a forward contract has an initial value of zero. Later it can have a positive or a negative value depending on changes in the price of the asset.

Forward Rate Agreement

Forward Rate Agreements (FRAs) are the most actively traded short term financial instrument other than exchange-traded futures and options. An FRA, which is the simplest of all the interest rate instruments, is a forward contract on interest rates. The buyers and sellers in an FRA are referred to as counterparties.

The FRA seller will receive a fixed interest payment and pay a floating interest payment. The FRA seller, also referred to as the receive fixed counterparty, expects interest rates to fall. The FRA buyer will receive a floating interest payment and pay a fixed interest payment. The FRA buyer, also referred to as the receive floating counterparty, expects interest rates to rise.

The FRA floating rate is usually LIBOR (London Interbank Offer Rate), but it could be the fed funds rate, the 90-day Treasury bill rate, the prime rate, or some other rate. Market convention for FRAs is to describe an FRA starting in three months and ending in six months as a 3X6 FRA, or threes-sixes. Numerous other combinations are possible (e.g., 1X4, 4X7, 6X12, 9X12, etc.) but the final maturity date on actively traded FRAs is no longer than 12 months.

The interest calculation for an FRA is similar to an interest rate swap. The *notional principal* is not actually paid but is simply the reference amount upon which interest is calculated. The difference between the fixed rate and the floating rate are settled in cash on the reset date (i.e., advanced settled) or the maturity date (i.e., settled in arrears). Whether advanced settled or settled in arrears, only the net cash flow is exchanged.

Similar to interest rate swaps, FRAs have credit risk, which is the risk that the counterparty fails to perform as contractually bound. To reduce this risk, an FRA contract can be advance settled. In addition, counterparties frequently exchange collateral with the other counterparty as surety to perform on the contract. FRAs can be custom designed to meet an institution's unique needs.

INTEREST RATE CAPS

An *interest rate cap* is designed to provide borrowers with protection against the rate of interest on a floating rate loan going above a specified rate level known as the *cap rate*. If the rate of interest on the loan does go above the cap rate, the seller of the cap pays the buyer the difference between the interest on the loan and the interest that would be required if the cap rate applied. Occasionally, caps are structured to guarantee that the average rate paid during the life of the loan, rather than the rate at any particular time, will not go above a certain level.

Interest rate caps are a type of over-the-counter interest rate option. A more precise mathematical characterization of a cap is as a portfolio series of put options on discount bonds. Similar to interest rate swaps, caps are offered principally by financial institutions. When a cap on a loan and the loan itself are both provided by the same financial institution, the cost of the options underlying the cap is often incorporated into the interest rate charged. When they are provided by different financial institutions, an up-front payment for the cap is likely to be required.

Caps would be an appropriate derivative instrument for liability-sensitive institutions wishing to hedge against rising interest rates.

INTEREST RATE FLOORS

An *interest rate floor* is designed to provide borrowers with protection against the rate of interest on a floating-rate loan going below a specified rate level. If the rate of interest on the loan does go below the *floor rate*, the seller of the floor pays the buyer the difference between the interest on the loan and the interest that would be required if the floor rate applied. A more precise mathematical characterization of a floor is as a portfolio of put options on interest rates or a portfolio of call options on discount bonds.

Interest rate floors would be useful to asset-sensitive financial institutions that want protection from falling interest rates. Because of market-driven "deposit floors," some institutions may be asset-sensitive under falling rates scenarios but be gap neutral or balanced under rising rate scenarios.

INTEREST RATE COLLARS

An *interest rate collar* specifies both the upper and lower limits for the rate that would be charged. An interest rate collar, which is sometimes referred to as a "floor-ceiling agreement" or a "range swap" is initially like an "out of the money" interest rate swap, because the collar agreement is activated only if rates move up or down by a predetermined level.

A collar is a combination of a long position in a cap and a short position in a floor. It is usually constructed so that the price of the cap equals the price of the floor. The net cost of the collar is then zero.

FUTURES CONTRACTS

Whereas cash markets provide investors with opportunities to trade Treasury securities for same-day or next-day delivery and payment, the Treasury futures market exists so that T-bills, notes, and bonds can be traded for deferred delivery and payment. Futures contracts are traded on an exchange such as the Chicago Board of Trade or the New York Futures Exchange. In practice, as little as 5 percent of futures contracts end up with the Treasury security actually being delivered. The futures contracts in Treasury securities include the following: three-month T-bill, two-year T-note, five-year T-note, ten-year T-note, and the thirty-year T-bond futures contract. The bill contract has a face value of $1 million per contract, while the others have a face value of $100,000.

Futures contracts are different from other securities in that they do not require an initial investment and are marked to market daily. Another distinguishing feature is that on the delivery date of the futures contract, the holder of a short futures contract has the right to choose which specific security to deliver against the contract. The cheapest bond that can be purchased would be delivered. This cheapest-to-deliver security feature of a futures contract leads to basis risk and an uncertain or dynamic duration of the futures contract, which can significantly affect hedge ratios and the performance of hedge activities.

Interest rate futures markets offer institutions that can forecast their future funding or lending needs the opportunity to lock in attractive interest rates when they become available. Futures contracts provide fixed-income portfolio managers with the opportunity to hedge against unfavorable interest rate movements.

Futures, and the corresponding cash price movements, are closely related. However, because participants in the cash and futures markets may have different objectives, there are times when the cash bond and futures contracts are trading at prices contrary to their expected relationship. Fixed-income arbitragers often seek out these situations and establish trading positions from which they will profit when the expected relationship between the cash and futures prices are eventually re-established.

T-bill futures can be used as a hedge against the flattening of the yield curve. For example, if the T-bill yield curve has a positive slope, an institution that has an investment horizon of three months has several alternatives. In addition to simply buying the three-month bill and holding it until maturity, the institution can *ride down the yield curve* by buying, for example, the six-month bill and selling it three months later. The latter strategy may produce superior results if the yield curve stays the same after three months, but if the yield curve shifts upward, the simple buy-and-hold strategy will produce better returns. In order to hedge against possible upward shifts in yields, the investor can buy the six-month bill and sell a T-bill futures contract that settles in three months. In a rising rate scenario, this strategy would outperform the buy-and-hold strategy without exposing the institution to the market-level risk of riding the yield curve.[10] However, as indicated above, if rates stay the same, the buy-and-hold strategy would outperform the hedge strategy by an amount equal to the cost of the futures contract.

It is important to recognize that futures hedging does not necessarily improve the total return of a transaction. In fact, a futures hedge will make the outcome worse roughly 50 percent of the time. What the futures hedge does do is reduce risk by making the outcome more certain.

OPTIONS

A *call (put) option* is an agreement granting the right to buy (sell) a fixed quantity of a bond or a bond future, at a specified price, for a specified period of time. The predetermined sale or purchase price of the underlying security is known as the *strike* or *exercise price*. An option contract is good only until its *expiration date*. If the buyer of the call (put) option can exercise his right to buy (sell) the underlying security on any date up to the expiration date, the option is said to be an *American* option; if it may only be exercised on the expiration date, it is said to be a *European* option.

Debt option contracts are commonly traded either on an exchange or over the counter (OTC). Options on T-bond and Treasury note (T-note) futures are traded on the Chicago Board of Trade, while cash bond options are traded on the American Stock Exchange and Chicago Board Options Exchange. The OTC market is a larger market than exchange traded options. Most OTC options are for terms of less than six months. OTC options include "optionlike" contracts, such as interest rate caps and floors and interest rate swaps.

One of the most important features of an option contract is that it guarantees the call (put) buyer a *right* to buy (sell) the underlying security at the agreed-upon strike price, but entails no *obligation* to do so. The seller of the option, also called the option writer, does have an obligation to sell (in the case of a call) or buy (in the case of a put) the underlying security at the agreed-upon strike price, upon demand (exercise) by the option holder.

Option Buyer

The most that the buyer of an option can lose is the cost of the option. The option buyer has no obligation to exercise the option and will do so only if there is a benefit.

The buyer of a call option has limited loss potential but unlimited gain potential. For example, if the price of the underlying bond remained below the strike price during the life of the option contract, the call would expire worthless, and the option buyer would have lost only the cost of the option. On the other hand, if the price of the underlying bond rises above the strike price, the call buyer would exercise the option, and the potential gains are (in theory) unlimited. Buying a call option is similar to buying the underlying security—it is a bullish strategy.

The buyer of a put option has limited loss potential and limited gain potential. For example, if the price of the bond falls to zero, the buyer of a put option has the right to sell the bond at the strike price. Thus, the potential gain to the buyer of a put option is limited to an amount equal to the strike price. The potential loss to the buyer of a put option cannot exceed the cost of the option. Buying a put option is similar to shorting the underlying security—it is a bearish strategy.

> *"The buyer of a call option has limited loss potential but unlimited gain potential."*

Option Seller

The most an option seller can gain is the amount of the option premium. On the other hand, the potential for losses is (in theory) unlimited. The option seller hopes that volatility remains low and the option expires unexercised, thereby resulting in an enhancement to portfolio income.

The seller of a call option is exposed to unlimited loss potential because of the obligation to sell the underlying security at the strike price regardless of its market price if and when the option is exercised. A call seller holding the underlying security on which the option is written is said to have written a *covered call*. A call seller not holding the underlying security on which the option is written is said to have written a *naked call*.

The seller of a put option is exposed to limited loss potential because if the price of the bond falls to zero, the seller of a put option is obligated to buy the bond at the strike price. Thus, the potential loss to the seller of a put option cannot exceed an amount equal to the strike price.

INTEREST RATE VOLATILITY AND THE INVESTMENT PORTFOLIO

There would be no need for this Chapter, or for that matter, this book, if we could accurately predict what interest rates will be tomorrow. Since the early 1970s, interest rate volatility has increased dramatically. Interest rate volatility seems to be the rule, rather than the exception. This volatility is driven by a variety of factors that are not likely to abate, including the following:

- Changes in Federal Reserve Board policies;

- International concerns about the relative strength or weakness of the U.S. dollar as compared to other major currencies;

- Shifts in economic strength throughout the world; and

- Debt and credit crises in world markets sparked by economic, political, and other factors.

In a mark-to-market environment, interest rate volatility causes volatility in the market value of available-for-sale securities and, therefore, shareholders' equity. Many financial institutions will attempt to manage interest rate volatility in concert with liquidity management through investment strategies that are overly "defensive." For example, an institution may attempt to mitigate the adverse effects of interest rate volatility by structuring a short-term, laddered investment portfolio that keeps the institution in the bond market at frequent intervals.

While this strategy may reduce capital volatility, it may *unnecessarily* reduce future investment activities. Larger institutions have adopted a more offensive approach, deploying the derivative instruments described above to mitigate the effects of interest rate volatility and protect the market value of investments.

In general terms, there are three methods used by financial institutions to manage interest rate risk through the investment portfolio:

- *Avoid Risk*—Institutions can avoid interest rate risk by investing in short-term securities. While this strategy will minimize gains and losses on securities, investing in short-term securities may actually increase interest rate risk if it causes an institution to become more interest rate sensitive.

- *Reduce Risk*—Institutions can choose investments as suggested by analysis of asset/liability management reports to manage the gap between interest-sensitive assets and liabilities.

- *Transfer Risk*—Institutions can transfer interest rate risk through the purchase and sale of derivative instruments to *hedge* interest rate risk.

HEDGING THE INVESTMENT PORTFOLIO

Hedging is a technique used to transfer risk. The Chicago Board of Trade defines hedging as, "the act of taking a temporary position in the futures market that is equal to and opposite to one's cash-market position to protect the cash position against loss due to price fluctuations."[11] This risk-transfer mechanism makes hedging a useful tool for managing interest rate risk.

Hedging involves risk-avoiders known as *hedgers* and risk-takers known as *speculators*. Hedgers and speculators are vital to the futures market. Hedgers are interested in reducing a risk that they already face. Whereas hedgers want to eliminate an exposure to movements in the price of an asset, speculators wish to take a position in the market. Either they are betting that a price will go up, or they are betting that it will go down. Speculators assume the risk that is transferred by hedgers. While the motive of the speculator is profit, speculators do provide an essential element to the marketplace—liquidity—that enables the hedger to buy or sell a large number of contracts without adversely disrupting the market.

In addition to hedgers and speculators, *arbitragers* are a third important group of participants in derivative securities markets. Arbitrage involves locking in a riskless profit by simultaneously entering into transactions in two or more markets. Arbitrage opportunities occur when the futures price of an asset gets out of line with its cash price.

In most situations, portfolio managers will be conducting their derivative activities as hedgers as opposed to speculators or arbitragers. In particular, portfolio managers will be attempting to protect the portfolio from losses on securities held in the available-for-sale category to reduce capital risk as described in Chapter 2. Be aware that bank regulators have indicated that derivative transactions intended for the purpose of speculating on price movements must be limited to institutions with derivative markets expertise and strong capital positions.

Hedge Strategies

There are two general types of hedges that institutions can use in managing the investment portfolio. The long hedge, sometimes called the *anticipatory hedge*, involves purchasing a futures contract or taking some other action as a temporary substitute for the purchase of the cash-market commodity at a later date. The purpose of the long hedge is to lock in a buying price. The short hedge, on the other hand, is initiated with a sale of a futures contract or some other action as a temporary substitute for a later cash market sale of the underlying asset. The purpose of the short hedge is to lock in a selling price.

Hedge strategies can be designed for "micro" hedges, which are put on for specific assets or liabilities, as well as "macro" hedges, which are structured to hedge the entire balance sheet. Generally accepted accounting principles (GAAP) requires that gains and losses on "micro" hedges be deferred and amortized over the life of the underlying asset or liability being hedged. GAAP requires that gains and losses on "macro" hedges be marked-to-market and recognized in current income.

The following strategies can help protect the market value of the investment portfolio during a rising rate environment. These strategies are especially important for securities included in the available-for-sale category where the institution is attempting to protect capital.

- *Sell Order*—While not a derivative instrument, an institution can place an order to sell a specific security if the price falls by a specified amount (e.g., 2 percent loss). If interest rates rise and the price of the security decreases to the strike point, the sale of the security would be triggered. It would not be practical to place sell orders on all of the securities in a portfolio. Transaction costs would be prohibitive, and the institution would still be faced with reinvestment risk. Moreover, such a move in interest rates may never take place. To protect against a *contingent* liability, the institution could resort to a *contingent instrument*—options.

- *Buy a Put Option*—The buyer of a put option has the right to sell a security at a specified price for a specified period of time if the price falls to a specified strike price. If interest rates rise, the increase in value of the put option will offset the decrease in value of the hedged securities. If interest rates do not rise, the loss is limited to the cost of the put option. This cost can be reduced somewhat by buying out-of-the-money put options because these options are much cheaper (in absolute price) than near-the-money options. At the same time, the percentage loss would be higher if rates do increase.

- *Buy an Interest Rate Cap*—Buy an "over-the-counter" interest rate option offered by financial institutions designed to hedge against interest rates rising above a certain level. If rates rise above the cap rate, the seller of the cap would pay the buyer under its obligation under the cap agreement. An "in-the-money" cap behaves like an interest rate swap, with the differential between the fixed and floating rates paid to the buyer of the cap.

- *Buy an Option to Buy a Cap*—Buy a caption, or an option to buy a cap. This would reduce the cost of insurance if it were ever needed, because the option would be cheaper than the actual cap, but it would raise the total cost if rates ever actually exceeded the cap's ceiling.

- *Sell a Covered Call Option*—This strategy provides no protection from a loss on the underlying security, but premiums from selling covered call options can partially offset these losses. The seller of a call option has the obligation to sell a security at a specified price for a specified period of time if the price falls to a specified strike price. Thus, the seller of a covered call gives up any potential profit from appreciation in the price of the underlying security above the strike price; in exchange, the seller receives the option price as a premium to enhance portfolio income.

The above strategies are examples of strategies used as insurance against investment portfolio losses during a rising rate environment. Keep in mind that the static hedging examples described above must be adjusted from time to time to reflect changes in the underlying investment portfolio (e.g., prepayments on mortgage securities and CMOs, called securities, step-ups, etc.). Strategies would be reversed to hedge against falling interest rates (e.g., place a buy order instead of a sell order; buy a call option instead of buy a put option, and so on.)

When interest rate volatility is high, or when matching maturities of three years or less, interest rate swap agreements are generally a more economic hedging technique than the use of financial futures or options.

Accounting for Hedges—GAAP

Included in the appendix to FASB Statement 115, Background Information and Basis for Conclusions, the FASB made the following comment regarding the use of hedge accounting:[12]

> This Statement does not address the accounting for other financial instruments used to hedge investments in securities. However, the accounting for those instruments may be affected if they are hedges of securities whose accounting is changed by this Statement. Gains and losses on instruments that hedge securities classified as trading would be reported in earnings, consistent with the reporting of unrealized gains and losses on the trading securities. Gains and losses on instruments that hedge available-for-sale securities are initially reported in a separate component of equity, consistent with the reporting for those securities, but then should be amortized as a yield adjustment. The reporting of available-for-sale securities at fair value does not change the recognition and measurement of interest income.

At one time, the FASB intended to include guidance on hedge accounting in Statement 115. In the April 16, 1993 draft of Statement 115, the following paragraph was included:[13]

> Hedging a debt security's interest rate risk or its foreign exchange risk prior to or concurrent with its classification as held-to-maturity is not inconsistent with the

asserted intent to hold the debt security to maturity. Thus a debt security that has been so hedged can be classified as held-to-maturity. However, because that classification is premised on an asserted intent to hold the security to maturity irrespective of subsequent changes in market interest rates, prepayment risk, or foreign exchange risk, it is inappropriate for an enterprise's financial reporting to reflect subsequent transactions as a hedge of a held-to-maturity security. Thus hedge accounting (that is deferring and amortizing the change in value due to changes in market interest rates, prepayment risk, or foreign exchange risk) may not be used for a financial instrument on the basis of its designation as a hedge of a held-to-maturity debt security subsequent to the debt security's classification in that category.

The above paragraph was deleted from the final pronouncement. However, the FASB has indicated that hedging will be revisited in the broader context of its Hedging Project.

Institutions should consult with their independent accountants to ascertain how Statement 115 will affect the accounting of existing or planned hedge products.

Accounting for Hedges—Tax

In October 1993, the Internal Revenue Service reversed a five-year-old position on the tax treatment of hedging transactions for banks and thrifts.[14] Under the new regulations, losses from most hedging transactions will be considered "ordinary" and, therefore, deductible from taxable income. Previously, the IRS had contended that such losses were "capital" and could be offset only against capital gains. This ordinary income treatment for hedges is important because if a financial institution incurred a loss on a hedge used to control its exposure to interest rate risk, and it was deemed a capital loss, the institution would not be able to realize the tax benefit of the hedge loss unless it had offsetting capital gains. As a general rule, financial institutions do not generate capital gains because most activities are taxed as ordinary.

The new regulations stipulate that hedges of an ordinary stream of income that flow from a capital asset will continue to generate a capital gain or loss. For example, an insurance company hedging the interest it earns on a bond it holds as a capital asset, will still generate capital gains or losses. In announcing the new regulations, Treasury officials indicated that Congress may

"Under the new regulations, losses from most hedging transactions will be considered "ordinary" and, therefore, deductible from taxable income."

decide to broaden what type of hedges qualify for ordinary income treatment. Until then, confusion will persist because a security held by a bank is considered to be an ordinary asset, while the same security held in the investment portfolio of an insurance company is considered to be a capital asset.

The new regulations require that transactions entered into beginning January 1, 1994, be identified as a hedge when the transaction is executed in order to receive ordinary treatment for tax purposes. Hedges in effect as of December 31, 1993, must be identified by March 31, 1994, to obtain ordinary income treatment.

The new regulations leave some questions unanswered. For example, it is not clear that all transactions (e.g., a hedge that converts a fixed-rate instrument into a floating rate) will be considered a hedging transaction. Accordingly, institutions should consult with their tax advisors for clarification on this and other issues.

DERIVATIVE ANALYTICS AND OPERATING SYSTEMS

Derivative analytics and operating systems are quite expensive. Many institutions initially start out with PC-based systems and/or adaptations of loan subsystems to control swaps and other interest rate agreements. Eventually, institutions out-grow these systems and opt for more expensive analytics and operating systems.

Strong internal controls and an adequate operating system are essential to the control of cash flows and proper accounting of derivatives. Unlike loans and deposits, which have simple monthly or quarterly interest accrual periods, derivative instruments can have complex accural features and accrual periods of six months or longer. In the case of caps, floors and collars, cash flows are not paid unless thresholds are triggered. Institutions should fully document accounting policies and procedures for derivative instruments before engaging in such activities.

SUMMARY

The increased use of derivative instruments is expected to continue as more institutions use these financial engineering tools to manage interest rate risk. The arrival of the mark-to-market era where institutions seek to protect the investment portfolio from erosion in market value will only hasten the use of these tools. Institutions must use caution to protect themselves against large losses resulting from counterparty failures or from adverse movements in market rates. Derivative products have become such useful tools to reduce interest rate risk that there is a growing belief among portfolio managers that the failure to use such products is speculative.

SUGGESTIONS FOR FURTHER READING

Burghardt, Galen, Morton Lane, and John Papa. *The Treasury Bond Basis: An In-Depth Analysis for Hedgers, Speculators, and Arbitragers.* Chicago: Probus Publishing Co., 1989.

CBOT Financial Instruments Guide. Chicago Board of Trade, 1987.

Commodity Trading Manual. Chicago Board of Trade, 1989.

Interest Rate Futures for Institutional Investors. Chicago Board of Trade, 1987.

Fabozzi, Frank J. and T. Dessa Fabozzi, *Bond Markets, Analysis, and Strategies.* Englewood Cliffs, NJ: Prentice Hall, 1989.

Fabozzi, Frank J., and Irving M. Pollack, eds. *Handbook of Fixed Income Securities.* 2nd. ed. Homewood, IL: Dow Jones-Irwin, 1986.

Figlewski, Stephen, William L. Silber, and Marti G. Subrahmanyam, eds. *Financial Options: From Theory to Practice.* Homewood, IL: Business One Irwin, 1990.

Hull, John C., *Options, Futures, and Other Derivative Securities.* Englewood Cliffs, NJ: Prentice-Hall, Inc., 1993.

Kolb, Robert W. *Understanding Futures Markets.* Glenview, IL: Scott Foresman, 1985.

Peck, A.E. ed. *Selected Writings on Futures Markets: Explorations in Financial Futures Markets.* Book V. Chicago: Chicago Board of Trade, 1985.

Rothstein, Nancy H., and James M. Little, eds. *The Handbook of Financial Futures.* New York: McGraw-Hill Book Company, 1984.

Stoll, Hans R., and Robert E. Whaley. *Futures and Options: Theory and Applications.* Cincinnati, OH: Southwestern Publishing Co., 1992.

The Journal of Derivatives. Published quarterly by Institutional Investors, Inc., New York, Volume 1, No. 1., Fall 1993.

Treasury Futures for Institutional Investors. Chicago Board of Trade, 1990.

The Delivery Process in Brief: Treasury Bond and Treasury Note Futures. Chicago Board of Trade, 1989.

Wong, M. Anthony, and Robert High, *Trading and Investing in Bond Options: Risk Management, Arbitrage, and Value Investing.* New York: John Wiley & Sons, 1991.

Both the Chicago Board of Trade and the Chicago Mercantile Exchange conduct seminars and have marketing and educational literature dealing with exchange-traded financial instruments. Mailing addresses and telephone numbers are as follows:

Chicago Board of Trade
LaSalle at Jackson
Chicago, IL 60604
Telephone: (800) THE-CBOT

The Chicago Mercantile Exchange
30 South Wacker Drive
Chicago, IL 60606
Telephone: (312) 930-1000

ENDNOTES

1. Speech by Eugene A. Ludwig, Comptroller of the Currency, delivered to the Institute of International Bankers, Washington, D.C., September 27, 1993.

2. *A National Survey of Chief Financial and Chief Investment Officers in 216 Financial Services Institutions,* Ernst & Young, 1993, p. 48.

3. *An Examiner's Guide to Investment Products and Practices* (Washington, D.C.: Comptroller of the Currency, Administrator of National Banks, December 1992), pp. 82-98.

4. Ibid., Eugene A. Ludwig speech, September 27, 1993.

5. Klinkerman, Steve. "Banc One's McCoy Tries to Calm Fears over Heavy Use of Derivatives." *American Banker,* October 22, 1993, p.4.

6. Ibid. p. 4.

7. Benton E. Gup and Robert Brooks, *Interest Rate Risk Management, The Banker's Guide to Using Futures, Options, Swaps and Other Derivative Instruments,* Chicago: Probus Publishing Company, pp. 141-142.

8. Ibid., pp. 142-143.

9. Hull, John C., *Options, Futures, and Other Derivative Securities.* Englewood Cliffs, NJ: Prentice Hall, p. 2.

10. Wong, M. Anthony, and Robert High, *Trading and Investing in Bond Options: Risk Management, Arbitrage, and Value Investing.* New York: John Wiley & Sons, Inc., pp. 33-34.

11. *CBOT Financial Instruments Guide* (Chicago, IL: Chicago Board of Trade, 1991), p. 4.

12. *Statement of Financial Accounting Standards No. 115, Accounting for Certain Investments in Debt and Equity Securities,* (Norwalk, CT: Financial Accounting Standards Board, May 1993), p. 38.

13. *Statement of Financial Accounting Standards, Accounting for Certain Investments in Debt and Equity Securities, April 16, 1993 Draft* (Norwalk, CT: Financial Accounting Standards Board), p. 5.

14. *The Wall Street Journal,* October 19, 1993, p. A2 and *Bloomberg Business News,* October 18, 1993.

Chapter 6: Accounting and Financial Reporting

Table of Contents—

Mark-to-Market Accounting Summary
  Held-to-Maturity Securities
  Trading Account Securities
  Available-for-Sale Securities
  Investment Transfers
  Impairment of Market Value
  Financial Statement Disclosures
Investment Portfolio Accounting—A History of Changes
Investment Accounting Systems
General Ledger Accounting
Regulatory Reporting
Income Tax Considerations
Summary

MARK-TO-MARKET ACCOUNTING SUMMARY

Statement 115 is effective for fiscal years beginning after December 15, 1993, although early adoption as of year-end 1993 is permitted. The goal of Statement 115 is not only to curtail gains trading, but also to improve financial reporting and standardize portfolio accounting practices across industry lines. Statement 115 applies to all commercial and industrial enterprises that invest in marketable securities, regardless of size, industry, financial/nonfinancial status. Statement 115 does not apply to not-for-profit organizations such as hospitals, colleges, and universities, religious institutions, trade associations, and private foundations. Also, Statement 115 does not apply to loans, leases, financial futures, options, swaps, and interest rate and foreign exchange rate agreements.

Statement 115 requires that investments securities be classified into one of three portfolios: *held-to-maturity, trading, and available-for-sale.* For reference purposes, Statement of Financial Accounting Standards No. 115, pages 1 to 11, are in Appendix B.

Held-to-Maturity Securities

Investments in debt securities are classified as *held-to-maturity* and recorded at amortized cost if the institution has the positive intent and ability to hold these securities to maturity. Statement 115 specifically prohibits an entity from classifying a debt security as held-to-maturity if the security may be sold in response to the following:

- Changes in market interest rates and related changes in the security's prepayment risk;

- Needs for liquidity;

- Changes in the availability of and the yield on alternative investments;

- Changes in funding sources and terms; or

- Changes in foreign currency risk.

Certain changes in circumstances allow a bank to sell investments without jeopardizing the held-to-maturity classification of similar securities. Permissible sales or transfers of held-to-maturity securities include the following situations:

- Evidence of a significant deterioration in the issuer's creditworthiness;

- A change in tax law that eliminates or reduces the tax-exempt status of interest on the debt security (but not a change in tax law that revises the marginal tax rates applicable to interest income);

- A major business combination or major disposition (such as sale of a segment) that necessitates the sale or transfer of held-to-maturity securities to maintain the enterprise's existing interest rate risk position or credit risk policy;

- A change in statutory or regulatory requirements significantly modifying either what constitutes a permissible investment or the maximum level of investments in certain kinds of securities, thereby causing an enterprise to dispose of a held-to-maturity security;

- A significant increase by the regulator in the industry's capital requirements that causes the enterprise to downsize by selling held-to-maturity securities;

- A significant increase in the risk weights of debt securities used for regulatory risk-based capital purposes; or

- Other isolated, nonrecurring, and unusual events that could not have been reasonably anticipated.

There are two exceptions in which a held-to-maturity security may be sold prior to final maturity without jeopardizing the held-to-maturity classification of other securities. The first occurs when the maturity or call date (if call is probable) is so close (e.g., three months) that interest rate risk is significantly reduced. The second exception occurs when the security has already returned at least 85 percent of the principal outstanding at acquisition due to either prepayments or scheduled payments.

Transfers of securities with significant deterioration of credit worthiness can occur prior to an actual downgrading in the issuer's published credit rating. Such a transfer must be in response to an actual deterioration in credit, not mere speculation. Deterioration should be supported with evidence about the issuers credit worthiness.

Trading Account Securities

Investments in *trading account* securities are reported at market value with unrealized gains and losses included in the income statement. The treatment of trading securities under Statement 115 is expected to be the same as the existing accounting for financial institutions.

Available-for-Sale Securities

Investments not classified as held-to-maturity or trading are classified as *available-for-sale* and reported at fair market value with unrealized gains/losses recorded (net of tax effect) as a separate component of equity.

Investment Transfers

Transfer of securities between categories are accounted for at fair market value. For transfers into the trading category, the unrealized holding gain or loss should be recognized in earnings. For other transfers, unrealized holding gains and losses should be reported as a separate component of shareholders' equity. Any unrealized gains and losses associated with transfers into the held-to-maturity category are reported as a separate component of shareholders' equity and should be amortized over the remaining life of the security as an adjustment to yield.

Figure 6.1 illustrates allowable transfers between available-for-sale, held-to-maturity, and trading categories.

> "Transfers of securities with significant deterioration of credit worthiness can occur prior to an actual downgrading in the issuer's published credit rating."

Figure 6.1 **TRANSFERS BETWEEN CATEGORIES**

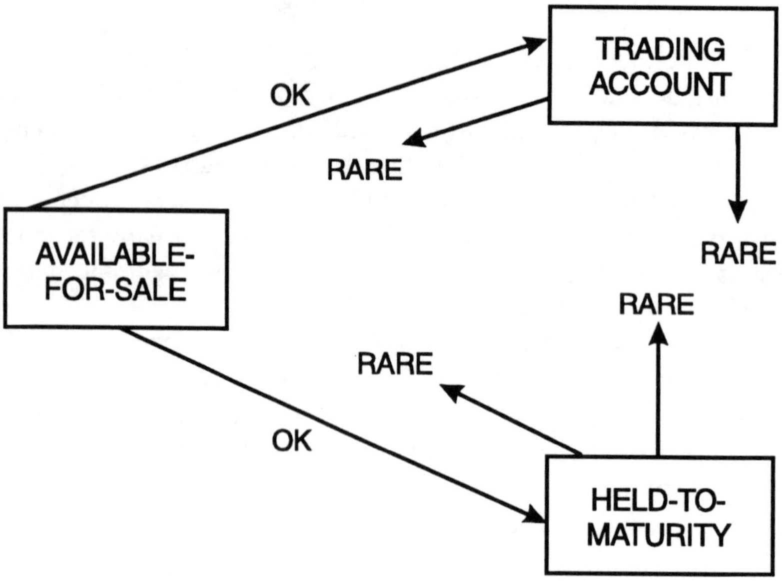

```
                        OK           TRADING
              ┌──────────────────▶   ACCOUNT
              │   ◀──────────────
              │        RARE              │
              │                          │ RARE
    AVAILABLE-│                          ▼
    FOR-SALE  │                        RARE
              │        RARE              ▲
              │   ◀──────────────        │
              │        OK                │
              └──────────────────▶    HELD-TO-
                                      MATURITY
```

Transfers from the held-to-maturity portfolio should be rare and Statement 115 requires specific disclosures of the transfer. Statement 115 indicates that "a pattern of sales or transfers of held-to-maturity securities is inconsistent with an expressed current intent to hold similar debt securities to maturity." Transfers from the trading account are rare because securities will be sold within a relatively short period of time. If such transfers do occur, they must be recorded at fair market value. Unlike transfers from the held-to-maturity category, however, transfers from the trading account do not involve the issue of tainting remaining securities in the category.

Impairment of Market Value

Statement 115 includes accounting and reporting guidance for securities with "impaired" values. If a decline in market values is considered to be other than temporary, the individual security should be written down to fair market value as a new cost basis. The amount of the write-down should be recognized in earnings as a realized loss.

Accounting literature indicates that for "investment in bonds and other investments with fixed maturity amounts, market declines may be considered temporary unless the evidence indicates that such investments will be disposed of before they mature or they may not be realizable." Thus, most changes in bond market values are considered to be "temporary." (Try telling that one to the boss.)

Financial Statement Disclosures

The following information should be disclosed in the notes to the financial statements for both held-to-maturity and available-for-sale investments:

- Aggregate fair market value;
- Gross unrealized holding gains and losses;
- Amortized cost basis by major security type; and
- Information on contractual maturities.

Statement 115 requires disclosure of the above information for the following security types:

- Equity securities;
- Treasury and Agency securities;
- State and municipal securities;
- Foreign securities;
- Corporate debt securities;
- Mortgage securities; and
- Other debt securities.

Other required financial statement disclosures include the following:

- The proceeds from sales of available-for-sale securities and gross realized gains and losses on those sales;
- The basis on which cost was determined in computing realized gain or loss;
- The gross gains and losses included in earnings from transfers of securities from available-for sale to trading;
- The change in net unrealized holding gain or loss on available-for-sale securities that has been included in the separate component of shareholders' equity during the period; and
- The change in net unrealized holding gain or loss on trading securities (held at period end) that has been included in earnings during the period.

Finally, for any sales of or transfers from securities classified as held-to-maturity, the amortized cost amount of the sold or transferred security, the related realized or unrealized gain or loss, and the circumstances leading to the decision to sell or

Table 6.1 Sample Footnote to Financial Statements

DRAFT OF CHANGES TO INVESTMENT SECURITY DISCLOSURE AS INTERPRETED FROM FASB 115

The aggregate book and market values of Held-To-Maturity and Available-For-Sale securities as of December 31, as well as gross unrealized gains and losses of investment securities were as follows:

HELD-TO-MATURITY	19x2 BOOK VALUE	UNREALIZED GAINS	UNREALIZED LOSSES	MARKET VALUE	19x1 BOOK VALUE	UNREALIZED GAINS	UNREALIZED LOSSES	MARKET VALUE
U.S. TREASURY AND OTHER U.S. GOVERNMENT AGENCIES	X,XXX,XXX	X,XXX,XXX	X,XXX,XXX	X,XXX,XXX	X,XXX,XXX	X,XXX,XXX	X,XXX,XXX	X,XXX,XXX
STATE AND MUNICIPAL	X,XXX,XXX	X,XXX,XXX	X,XXX,XXX	X,XXX,XXX	X,XXX,XXX	X,XXX,XXX	X,XXX,XXX	X,XXX,XXX
MORTGAGE-BACKED	X,XXX,XXX	X,XXX,XXX	X,XXX,XXX	X,XXX,XXX	X,XXX,XXX	X,XXX,XXX	X,XXX,XXX	X,XXX,XXX
CORPORATE DEBT	X,XXX,XXX	X,XXX,XXX	X,XXX,XXX	X,XXX,XXX	X,XXX,XXX	X,XXX,XXX	X,XXX,XXX	X,XXX,XXX
FOREIGN GOVERNMENT DEBT	X,XXX,XXX	X,XXX,XXX	X,XXX,XXX	X,XXX,XXX	X,XXX,XXX	X,XXX,XXX	X,XXX,XXX	X,XXX,XXX
OTHER	X,XXX,XXX	X,XXX,XXX	X,XXX,XXX	X,XXX,XXX	X,XXX,XXX	X,XXX,XXX	X,XXX,XXX	X,XXX,XXX
TOTAL	X,XXX,XXX	X,XXX,XXX	X,XXX,XXX	X,XXX,XXX	X,XXX,XXX	X,XXX,XXX	X,XXX,XXX	X,XXX,XXX

AVAILABLE-FOR-SALE	19x2 BOOK VALUE	UNREALIZED GAINS	UNREALIZED LOSSES	MARKET VALUE	19x1 BOOK VALUE	UNREALIZED GAINS	UNREALIZED LOSSES	MARKET VALUE
U.S. TREASURY AND OTHER U.S. GOVERNMENT AGENCIES	X,XXX,XXX	X,XXX,XXX	X,XXX,XXX	X,XXX,XXX	X,XXX,XXX	X,XXX,XXX	X,XXX,XXX	X,XXX,XXX
STATE AND MUNICIPAL	X,XXX,XXX	X,XXX,XXX	X,XXX,XXX	X,XXX,XXX	X,XXX,XXX	X,XXX,XXX	X,XXX,XXX	X,XXX,XXX
MORTGAGE-BACKED	X,XXX,XXX	X,XXX,XXX	X,XXX,XXX	X,XXX,XXX	X,XXX,XXX	X,XXX,XXX	X,XXX,XXX	X,XXX,XXX
CORPORATE DEBT	X,XXX,XXX	X,XXX,XXX	X,XXX,XXX	X,XXX,XXX	X,XXX,XXX	X,XXX,XXX	X,XXX,XXX	X,XXX,XXX
FOREIGN GOVERNMENT DEBT	X,XXX,XXX	X,XXX,XXX	X,XXX,XXX	X,XXX,XXX	X,XXX,XXX	X,XXX,XXX	X,XXX,XXX	X,XXX,XXX
EQUITY	X,XXX,XXX	X,XXX,XXX	X,XXX,XXX	X,XXX,XXX	X,XXX,XXX	X,XXX,XXX	X,XXX,XXX	X,XXX,XXX
OTHER	X,XXX,XXX	X,XXX,XXX	X,XXX,XXX	X,XXX,XXX	X,XXX,XXX	X,XXX,XXX	X,XXX,XXX	X,XXX,XXX
TOTAL	X,XXX,XXX	X,XXX,XXX	X,XXX,XXX	X,XXX,XXX	X,XXX,XXX	X,XXX,XXX	X,XXX,XXX	X,XXX,XXX

The amortized cost and estimated market value of Held-To-Maturity and Available-For-Sale securities at December 31, 19x2, by contractual maturity, are shown below. Expected maturities may differ from contractual maturities because borrowers may have the right to call or prepay obligations with or without call or prepayment penalties.

HELD-TO-MATURITY	BOOK VALUE	MARKET VALUE
DUE IN ONE YEAR OR LESS	X,XXX,XXX	X,XXX,XXX
DUE AFTER ONE YEAR THROUGH FIVE YEARS	X,XXX,XXX	X,XXX,XXX
DUE AFTER FIVE YEARS THROUGH TEN YEARS	X,XXX,XXX	X,XXX,XXX
DUE AFTER TEN YEARS	X,XXX,XXX	X,XXX,XXX
SUBTOTAL	X,XXX,XXX	X,XXX,XXX
NO CONTRACTUAL MATURITY	X,XXX,XXX	X,XXX,XXX
TOTAL	X,XXX,XXX	X,XXX,XXX

AVAILABLE-FOR-SALE	BOOK VALUE	MARKET VALUE
DUE IN ONE YEAR OR LESS	X,XXX,XXX	X,XXX,XXX
DUE AFTER ONE YEAR THROUGH FIVE YEARS	X,XXX,XXX	X,XXX,XXX
DUE AFTER FIVE YEARS THROUGH TEN YEARS	X,XXX,XXX	X,XXX,XXX
DUE AFTER TEN YEARS	X,XXX,XXX	X,XXX,XXX
SUBTOTAL	X,XXX,XXX	X,XXX,XXX
NO CONTRACTUAL MATURITY	X,XXX,XXX	X,XXX,XXX
TOTAL	X,XXX,XXX	X,XXX,XXX

During 19x2, $xxx,xxx of Held-To-Maturity securities were sold as a result of a significant deterioration in the creditworthiness of the issuer. Losses of $xxx,xxx were realized on these sales. There were no transfers from Held-To-Maturity securities during 19x2. There were no sales or transfers from Held-To-Maturity securities in 19x1 or 19x0.

Proceeds from sales of Available-For-Sale securities for the three years ended December 31, 19x2, as well as gross gains and losses realized on these sales were as follows:

	19x2	19x1	19x0
Proceeds	X,XXX,XXX	X,XXX,XXX	X,XXX,XXX
Gross Gains	X,XXX,XXX	X,XXX,XXX	X,XXX,XXX
Gross Losses	X,XXX,XXX	X,XXX,XXX	X,XXX,XXX

The gross gains and losses included in earnings from transfers of Available-For-Sale securities into the Trading category for the three years ended December 31, 19x2, were as follows:

	19x2	19x1	19x0
Gross Gains	X,XXX,XXX	X,XXX,XXX	X,XXX,XXX
Gross Losses	X,XXX,XXX	X,XXX,XXX	X,XXX,XXX

Revised Accounting Policy Statement

The appropriate classification of securities is determined at the time of purchase and is re-evaluated at each balance sheet date. Gains or losses on the sale of securities are recognized on a specific identification, trade-date basis. Transfers of securities between the classifications are made at fair value.

Securities held-to-maturity are acquired with the ability and intent to hold such securities until maturity. These securities are carried at amortized cost adjusted for amortization of premium and accretion of discount, computed by the interest method. The amortized cost of the specific security sold is used to compute gains or losses on the sale of investment securities.

Marketable equity securities and debt securities not classified as held-to-maturity are classified as available-for-sale. Securities available-for-sale are acquired as part of the corporation's asset/liability management strategy and may be sold in response to changes in interest rates, changes in prepayment risk and other factors. Securities available-for-sale are carried at fair value, with unrealized gains based on the difference between amortized cost and market value, reported as a separate component of shareholders' equity, net-of-tax. The amortized cost of debt securities in this category is adjusted for amortization of premiums and accretion of discounts to maturity and is included in interest income. Realized gains and losses and declines in value judged to be other-than-temporary on these securities are included in securities gains and losses. Related interest and dividends are included in interest income.

Trading account assets are held with the intent of selling them at a profit and are carried at market. Adjustments to market value are included in "trading account profits" in the consolidated statement of income. Trading account assets are comprised primarily of securities backed by the U.S. Treasury and various federal agencies.

transfer the security shall be disclosed in the notes to the financial statements for each period for which the results of operations are presented.

The disclosures indicated above are illustrated on Table 6.1, Sample Footnote to Financial Statements.

INVESTMENT PORTFOLIO ACCOUNTING— A HISTORY OF CHANGES

Institutions have a long history of learning to cope with changes in generally accepted accounting principles (GAAP), taxation, and regulatory and financial reporting. This history gives some insight as to how institutions may change their investment management in response to Statement 115.

During the 1950s, when Treasury interest rates were 1 to 2 percent, GAAP required an institution to amortize the premium on a bond, the same as today's accounting. However, accretion of discounts had not yet become GAAP. Initially, institutions recorded only the bond coupon as income, with the discount taken into earnings at maturity. Because of this accounting treatment, discount issues initially earned less than par and premium bonds with similar yields and, therefore, they traded somewhat cheap to the market on a yield-to-maturity basis. In the late 1950's, GAAP changed as institutions such as Irving Trust and Wachovia began to accrete the discount into current earnings. As other institutions followed this lead, it did not take long for the market-yield disparity on discount bonds to disappear.

Prior to 1983, institutions reported gains and losses on the sale of securities as a separate line item (net of tax) *after* net income after taxes. This financial reporting was somewhat like the current financial statement reporting of an extraordinary item. By reporting "core" earnings (net income after taxes) separate from securities gains and losses, analysts and other users of financial statements were better able to assess the performance of an institution.

Some institutions used this dual bottom line to "manipulate" earnings. For example, a portfolio manager could complete an investment swap by selling securities at losses and reinvesting the proceeds at prevailing higher yields. Securities losses would reduce retained earnings in the year of the swap. However, the investment portfolio would be better positioned to contribute to the net margin and core earnings in future years.

When the financial reporting of securities gains and losses changed to the single bottom line currently used, bank analysts and other users of financial statements continued to separate

> *"Some institutions used this dual bottom line to "manipulate" earnings."*

securities transactions from core earnings. This analysis is especially important for certain institutions which have a history of *gains trading*, the practice of overstating net income by taking investment gains into earnings but deferring losses. Gains trading often hides deeper underlying credit problems. It was because of this gains trading issue that regulators and the Securities and Exchange Commission pressured the FASB into issuing Statement 115.

Back in the 1960s, when the corporate income tax was 48 percent, gains on the sale of securities were taxed as capital gains at a rate of one-half of the ordinary income tax rate. However, losses on the sale of securities were taxed at a rate of 48 percent. This tax treatment was extremely favorable for institutions because gains could be taxed at 24 percent in "gain years" and losses could be taxed at a benefit of 48 percent in "loss years". In the gain years, institutions would avoid booking losses, preferring to pay taxes at the capital gains rate of 24 percent. In the loss years, institutions would avoid booking gains, preferring to accrue a tax benefit at a rate of 48 percent. The capital gains tax was changed in 1969.

Prior to the 1980s, tax-free securities represented approximately 40 percent of total investment securities. Beginning with TEFRA in 1982 and culminating with the Tax Reform Act of 1986, Congress passed legislation to reduce the tax benefits of owning tax-free securities with the goal of making institutions pay the Alternative Minimum Tax. As a result of this legislation, institutions reduced the purchase of tax-free investments, which now represent about 10 percent of total investment securities. Institutions have replaced tax-free securities with mortgage securities, which now account for nearly one-half of the investment portfolio. The advent of mortgage securities, and the complexities of accounting for discounts and premiums related thereto, caused a change described in the following paragraph.

In 1987, generally accepted accounting principles were refined to require institutions to follow the constant yield method of accounting for premiums and discounts on investment securities. This change in accounting was necessary, in part, to respond to the proliferation of mortgage securities. Because of uncertain prepayments and average lives, and the complication of accounting for discounts or premiums, yields reported on the same mortgage security could be different from institution to institution. The constant yield method of accounting provided much needed guidance for institutions to consistently account for mortgage securities and other investment products. The constant yield method of accounting required costly updates to investment accounting systems. Similarly, investment accounting systems must be updated to satisfy management reporting requirements of Statement 115.

In addition to generally accepted accounting principles, regulatory reporting of investment securities has also influenced the management of the investment portfolio. Beginning in 1992, institutions have followed risk-based capital guidelines, which assign risk-weights to assets based on relative credit strength. Risk-weights vary from zero for direct obligations of the U.S. government (including GNMAs) to 100 percent for corporate securities. Mortgages securitized by an agency of the U.S. government (FNMA or FHLMC) have a risk-weight of 20 percent, whereas qualifying residential mortgages have a risk-weight of 50 percent. Collateralized mortgage obligations have the same risk-weights of the underlying collateral. Particularly for thinly capitalized institutions, these risk-weights have influenced the selection of investment securities with an emphasis on low risk-weight investments.

Investment portfolio managers are accustomed to changing investment markets and, as chronicled above, the changing rules of accounting for investments. Statement 115 changes the rules of the game once again. The onslaught of accounting and regulatory guidelines will continue. Currently, two additional regulations are in the works—measurement of interest rate risk (FFIEC) and accounting for off-balance sheet transactions (FASB). Some of the changes described above occurred even though there was no industry consensus (as in the case of Statement 115). Some say that Statement 115 is a compromise or piecemeal solution where the medicine is worse than the disease. Time will tell.

INVESTMENT ACCOUNTING SYSTEMS

Never before has the investment manager had to juggle so many requirements to successfully manage the portfolio. The investment manager must now purchase the right bond, at the right time, for the right purpose, at the right price, and with the advent of Statement 115, place it in the right investment category. Add to these requirements the current economic environment of weak loan demand, low interest rates, and disintermediation of bank deposits and the result is that much greater demands will be placed on investment accounting systems.

Obviously, investment accounting systems must be revised to satisfy financial reporting requirements for held-to-maturity, trading, and available-for-sale categories. These disclosure requirements are illustrated on Table 6.1, Sample Footnote to Financial Statements. To provide information for new general

"Never before has the investment manager had to juggle so many requirements to successfully manage the portfolio."

ledger accounts, many routine investment management reports, such as bond discount and premium journals, and book value and market value reports, must be revised to report both held-to-maturity and available-for-sale categories. Bond accounting systems must be updated to include new data fields for transfer date, previous market value, realized gain (loss) and unrealized gain (loss). A new transaction journal must be prepared to document transfers between categories and to provide an audit trail for independent accountants and bank examiners to validate that transfers were made for permissible reasons.

Be aware that the bond accounting systems used by many institutions today are based on a 1960s batch processing technology. Some of these systems have not been updated to efficiently handle the accounting and analysis of new investment products such as mortgage securities. Institutions should question their bond accounting vendors about plans for updating these systems to ensure that required management information and financial statement disclosures are readily available upon adopting Statement 115.

During the 1980s, many institutions purchased personal computer (PC)-based investment accounting programs. These accounting programs are somewhat expensive but they are popular with accounting departments because custom reporting features make it easier to close the books at month-end. These systems have one major fault—the difficulty of obtaining timely and accurate bond pricing. Such programs rely on costly dial-up pricing services, which reduce the cost savings of PC-based systems. In lieu of dial-up pricing, institutions frequently rely on time-consuming dealer pricing, which may not be deemed to be an independent source by independent accountants. Service bureau providers of investment accounting systems, such as Wachovia's Investment Management Service, balance the needs of comprehensive management reporting, independent pricing, accurate accounting and reasonable cost.

GENERAL LEDGER ACCOUNTING

Unfortunately, Statement 115 will require most institutions to double or even triple the number of general ledger accounts required to account for investment securities.

Institutions that expect to have significant available-for-sale securities may wish to establish a new set of accounts (i.e., par value, premiums, discounts, accrued interest, interest, amortization, and accretion) for each security type for both available-for-sale and held-to-maturity categories. By establishing new sets of accounts, the "old" general ledger accounts can be maintained to preserve historical budget and actual investment balances. Under this general ledger structure, instead of one set of accounts for each security type, an institution would have three sets of accounts, two new sets and one old set.

Alternatively, for institutions that will classify most of their investments as held-to-maturity, institutions may wish to establish one set of general ledger accounts for the new available-for-sale category. Most investments would remain in the held-to-maturity category and would be recorded in the renamed old general ledger accounts. If available-for-sale investments are purchased, they would be recorded in new general ledger accounts as needed. This structure reduces the number of general ledger accounts but it may contribute to some confusion over comparability of general ledger accounts, or lack thereof, for prior period and budget comparisons.

In addition to the investment general ledger accounts described above, a *market valuation adjustment account* must be established for each security type in the available-for-sale category. This account will be used to record the aggregate difference between book value and market value of available-for-sale investments. At each valuation date, this account should be reconciled to the investment accounting system.

An *unrealized gain and loss equity account* must be established for inclusion in stockholders' equity. This general ledger control account is used to record the offset (net of tax) of the market valuation adjustment account for unrealized gains and losses for investments in the available-for-sale category described above. Separate *deferred tax accounts* must be established to control deferred tax debits and credits related to the market valuation adjustment account.

Finally, if an available-for-sale security is transferred to the held-to-maturity category, a separate *unrealized gain or loss equity transfer account* must be established to record the unrealized holding gain or loss at the date of the transfer. This account will continue to be reported in shareholders' equity with the balance in this equity valuation account amortized over the remaining life of the security as an adjustment of yield in a manner consistent with the amortization of any premium or discount.

It is important for institutions to reconcile the general ledger balances to the investment accounting system at each valuation date to maintain the integrity of the investment categories reported under Statement 115.

Finally, at most institutions, the market values of investment securities are not under general ledger control. However,

Table 6.2 Accounting Journal Entries

BALANCE SHEET	Note A Starting 1/01/94	Note B 3/31/94	Note C 6/30/94	Note D 9/30/94	Note E 12/31/94	Note F 3/31/95	Note G 6/30/95	Note H Ending 9/30/95
Investments								
Held-to-Maturity	$100,000	$ 51,000			$50,000	$(50,000)	$(50,000)	$101,000
Market Valuation					1,000			1,000
Available-for-Sale	50,000	51,000		$(50,000)	(51,000)		50,000	50,000
Market Valuation	1,000		$2,000	(2,000)	(1,000)		(2,000)	(2,000)
Trading Account	100,000	(100,000)		50,000		40,000		90,000
Total Investments	$251,000	$ 2,000	$2,000	$ (2,000)	$ (1,000)	$(10,000)	$ (2,000)	$240,000
Liabilities								
Current Taxes Payable		$ 700				$ (3,500)		$ (2,800)
Deferred Taxes	$ 350		$ 700	$ (700)	$ (350)		$ (700)	(700)
Stockholders' Equity								
Unrealized Gain (Loss)	650		1,300	(1,300)	(650)		(1,300)	(1,300)
Retained Earnings		1,300				(6,500)		(5,200)
Liabilities and Stockholders' Equity	$1,000	$2,000	$2,000	$(2,000)	$(1,000)	$(10,000)	$ (2,000)	$(10,000)
INCOME STATEMENT								
Trading Gain (Loss)		$2,000				$(10,000)		$(8,000)
Tax Provision (Benefit)		700				(3,500)		(2,800)
Net Income (Loss)	$ 0	$1,300	$ 0	$ 0	$ 0	$ (6,500)	$ 0	$(5,200)

100 Chapter 6

such general ledger control may now be advisable since market value accounting will be reported in the financial statements, not just the footnotes. Independent accountants will now scrutinize these market values more closely. And the general ledger is a more permanent document for these important financial records.

Table 6.2, Accounting Journal Entries illustrates the accounting impact of certain investment securities transactions, including transfers and valuation accounting.

Note A—Initial Adoption of Statement 115

Record available-for-sale securities at 102. Record book value of held-to-maturity securities; market value of held-to-maturity securities at 102 disclosed in notes to financial statements. Record book and market value of trading securities at 100.

Note B—Transfer from Trading to Available-for-Sale and Held-to-Maturity

Record transfer of securities from trading account to held-to-maturity and available-for-sale at fair market value of 102. Previously unrealized gain of $2,000 recorded during the quarter ending March 31, 1994, should *not* be reversed from earnings. Book value of available-for-sale and held-to-maturity securities is fair market value on the date of transfer. Transfers from trading account should be rare.

Note C—Record Quarterly Valuation of Available-for-Sale

Record increase in market value of available-for-sale securities during the quarter ending June 30, 1994, using the market valuation adjustment account. This valuation adjustment must be recorded at each reporting date.

Note D—Transfer from Available-for-Sale to Trading Account

Record transfer of available-for-sale security (original book value of 100; market value of 104 at June 30, 1994) to trading account at fair market value 100. Previously reported market valuation adjustment account and related unrealized gain or loss equity account and deferred tax accounts must be reversed. Transfers from trading account should be rare.

Note E—Transfer from Available-for-Sale to Held-to-Maturity

Record transfer of available-for-sale security (original book value of 102; market value of 104 at September 30, 1994) to held-to-maturity at fair market value of 102. Unrealized gain of $650 previously recorded as unrealized gain or loss equity account remains in stockholders' equity in separate unrealized gain or loss equity *transfer* account and should be amortized as a yield adjustment over the remaining life of the security in a manner consistent with the amortization of the $1,000 premium. Held-to-maturity valuation transfer account of $1,000 should be amortized separately from other premiums or discounts.

Note F—Transfer from Held-to-Maturity to Trading Account

Record transfer of securities from held-to-maturity to trading account at fair market value of 90. Transfers should be rare (e.g., significant deterioration in the creditworthiness of a municipal credit). Report at fair market value. Unrealized gains or losses should be reported in earnings.

Note G—Transfer from Held-to-Maturity to Available-for-Sale

Record transfer of securities from held-to-maturity to available-for-sale. Transfers should be **rare** (e.g., acquisition of institution requiring possible sale of investments to maintain interest rate risk position). Report difference between book value and fair market value in the market valuation adjustment account.

Note H—Ending Balances

Ending general ledger control balances must be reconciled monthly to the investment accounting system and to underlying current and deferred tax liability records. Specifically, the available-for-sale market valuation adjustment account must be reconciled to the unrealized gain or loss equity account and related deferred tax liability accounts (federal and state).

REGULATORY REPORTING

By law, regulatory agencies require that regulatory financial statements be prepared in accordance with generally accepted accounting principles. Regulatory agencies have indicated they will adopt Statement 115 for regulatory reporting. However, regulators have not yet issued final guidelines on Statement 115.

The most significant issue that regulators must decide is whether to include unrealized gains and losses in the definition of risk-based regulatory capital (commonly referred to as "Tier II" capital). Statement 115 would not be the first difference between GAAP and RAP capital calculations. Regulatory capital differs from GAAP equity capital for numerous other reasons including the following:

Additions—
- Some or all of the allowance for loan losses.
- Certain subordinated debt.
- Minority interest in certain subsidiaries.

Deductions—
- Goodwill and certain identifiable intangible assets.
- Investment in certain unconsolidated subsidiaries.

If regulators exclude unrealized gains and losses from the definition of risk-based regulatory capital, capital volatility would be reduced. Institutions could then take a little more market risk in the available-for-sale portfolio. Capital volatility can be a problem for institutions because the Federal Deposit Insurance Corporation Improvement Act of 1991 (FDICIA) requires bank regulators to take certain actions and restrict bank activities based on the institution's capital level.

FDICIA establishes five capital zones and requires regulators to take increasingly stringent actions if an institution's capital level falls into particular zones. These actions include dividend and growth restriction, and extend to closing institutions with tangible equity below 2 percent of assets.

The capital volatility that may result from Statement 115 could result in an immediate earnings impact in the form of higher FDIC premiums, which are based on an institution's level of capital. For example, a one-day swing in interest rates at year end that caused a "well capitalized" bank, with $10 billion in insured deposits, to fall to "adequately capitalized," could cause the institution's FDIC premiums to increase by $1.5 million for the next six months.[1]

Many institutions will likely protect themselves from this risk by either reducing potential capital volatility (by shortening the life of their investment securities or increasing hedging activity) or by maintaining a larger capital cushion.

Institutions should be aware that Regulatory agencies were initially opposed to mark-to-market accounting requirements.

The Office of the Comptroller of the Currency (OCC) responded to the exposure draft of Statement 115, commenting:[2]

> We believe that the proposed held-to-maturity criteria are so stringent that most of a bank's investment portfolio will be required to be classified as available-for-sale and carried at fair value. The overly stringent nature of these criteria is reinforced by the Board's position that "an entity's decision to hold a security to maturity implies that the entity has chosen to disregard the effects of changes in both market interest rates and the security's prepayment risk during the term of the security." *Prudent bank managers cannot and should not disregard the effects of changes in market factors on those securities that they intend to hold to maturity.*

The OCC has not yet issued its guidelines for reviewing compliance with Statement 115. However, the OCC's comments above give some insight as to how bank examiners might review the classification of investments in the held-to-maturity and available-for-sale categories.

In addition to the classification of investments, regulators have been concerned about the volatility of capital resulting from available-for-sale investments. As discussed in Chapter 1, institutions would be wise to view this capital with caution. Mark-to-market capital can disappear quickly in a bear market. For the regulators, it will be a case of, "Heads I win, tails you lose." Institutions will be cautioned against leveraging this capital too much in a bull market, and will face the consequences of FDICIA in a bear market.

INCOME TAX CONSIDERATIONS

Unrelated to Statement 115, effective January 1, 1993 for calendar year taxpayers, the Omnibus Budget Reconciliation Act of 1993 (OBRA '93) includes a "mark-to-market" provision that may require dealers in securities to pay more income taxes.

Table 6.3 Book and Tax Mark-to-Market Comparison

FASB Statement No. 115		Omnibus Budget Reconciliation Act of 1993	
Type of Security	**Carrying Value**	**Type of Security**	**Inventory Value**
Held-to-Maturity	Amortized Cost	Held-for-Investment	Cost
Available-for-Sale	Mark-to-Market	Not-Held-for-Sale	Cost
Trading Account	Mark-to-Market	Held-for-Sale	Mark-to-market

While a commercial bank may not be a dealer in securities for other purposes, the terms "dealer" and "securities" are broadly defined in the Act to include some common banking activities. For example, Congressional reports on OBRA '93 define a "dealer" to include an institution that originates and sells mortgage loans. The definition of "securities" includes: stock and other registered securities; notes, bonds, debentures, and any other evidence of indebtedness; notional principal contracts based on interest rates, currency, or equities; and any evidence of an interest in a derivative of such, security, as well as any clearly identified hedge of such a security.

OBRA '93 requires that dealers in securities to mark their inventory of Held-for-Sale securities and hedges of those securities to market and include any gains or losses in income. Prior to 1993, if a dealer used the cost method or lower of cost or market (LOCOM) method for inventory valuation, taxes on unrealized gains were deferred until the securities were sold. Generally, gains and losses resulting from this mark-to market provision will be taxed as ordinary, not capital. Any net income or loss resulting from the mark-to-market adjustment for the Held-for-Sale portfolio held as of January 1, 1993 will be spread over five years.

For tax purposes, there are three designations for "securities" as defined by the IRS; *held-for-investment, not-held-for-sale* and *held-for-sale*. The tax and book accounting for these categories is illustrated on Table 6.3. Institutions should review applicable financial instruments including loans, trading and investment securities, notional principal contracts and derivative instruments, and indicate which securities will be marked-to-market (Held-for-Sale category). If clearly identified on their books and records, and documented by October 31, 1993, institutions will be exempt from the mark-to-market tax treatment for securities classified as either held-for-investment, or not-held-for sale (for loans). If not properly identified, all securities held by a dealer are subject to mark-to-market treatment and the penalty provisions of OBRA '93 may apply.

OBRA '93 provides no guidance on how to designate the tax category of a security. Designation in the Investment Committee minutes or in a policy statement from the Chief Financial Officer may suffice. Institutions must be careful to clearly document the tax and book designations of investment and trading securities. OBRA '93 requires that proper designation must be made generally at the time of purchase of each security.

Confusion may exist because the *available-for-sale* (GAAP) and the *held-for-sale* (tax) categories have similar names and, as illustrated on Table 6.3, both follow mark-to-market accounting.

"Generally, gains and losses resulting from this mark-to market provision will be taxed as ordinary, not capital."

However, most institutions will classify available-for-sale securities in either the not-held-for-sale category or the held-for-investment category for tax purposes and thereby avoid mark-to-market accounting treatment. Thus, an available-for-sale security could be valued for book purposes at mark-to-market but valued for tax purposes at cost.

SUMMARY

Never before has the investment manager had to juggle so many requirements to successfully manage the portfolio. The investment manager must purchase the right bond, at the right time, for the right purpose, at the right price, and place it in the right category. Prior to the issuance of Statement 115, the accounting for the investment portfolio was relatively simple. Now institutions will double or triple the number of general ledger accounts. And, with the Omnibus Budget Reconciliation Act of 1993, institutions must keep two sets of books—one for financial reporting and one for tax reporting. With these added burdens of accounting, regulatory, and tax reporting, institutions should closely review the investment accounting and financial reporting requirements of Statement 115.

ENDNOTES

1. *A National Survey of Chief Finanical and Chief Investment Officers in 216 Financial Services Institutions,* Ernst & Young, 1993, p. 13.

2. Comment letter from Comptroller of the Currency, Administrator of National Banks, to the Financial Accounting Standards Board, January 12, 1993, p. 1.

Chapter 7: Investment Management Policy and Documentation

Table of Contents—

Investment Policy
Illustrative Investment Policy
Authorized Investments
Classification of Investment Securities
    Held-to-Maturity Securities
    Trading Account Securities
    Available-for-Sale Securities
Transfer Between Categories of Investment
Unsuitable Investment Practices
Selection of Security Dealers
Duties and Responsibilities
    Investment Officer
    Investment Management Committee
Investment Trade Documentation

INVESTMENT POLICY

The investment policy lays the foundation for the successful management of the investment portfolio. In connection with the adoption of Statement 115, investment managers should update the institution's investment policy and seek management's input in the oversight of investment activities. Chapter 7 examines what should be included in an investment policy, including duties and responsibilities of the investment officer and the investment management committee.

The following investment policy was prepared for an institution with total assets in excess of $30 billion. Certain investment activities included herein may not be appropriate for your institution. However, for most institutions, this illustrative policy provides a comprehensive reference for use in updating their investment policies and procedures for the requirements of both Statement 115 and Banking Circular 228.

> *"In updating the investment policy, institutions must determine the level of detail to be included in the policy."*

In addition to updating the investment policy, institutions should bolster compliance efforts to ensure that investment policies are being carried out in accordance with management objectives. In the past, internal auditors and independent accountants have performed largely substantive year-end audit procedures in the investment portfolio. As a result, this oversight of the investment policy has been somewhat superficial.

However, Statement 115 invokes greater documentation requirements for the investment portfolio manager. Purchases and sales of investment securities must be well documented and recorded in the right category. Transfers of securities between categories can be made only for permissible reasons. The risk of tainting the held-to-maturity portfolio because of an ill-advised sale or transfer requires management to be more vigilant about enforcing investment policies. In short, managing the investment portfolio under Statement 115 will require more teamwork than in the past. In addition to investment management, the team should include the controller's department, internal audit and the independent accountants.

In updating the investment policy, institutions must determine the level of detail to be included in the policy. Some institution's prefer a "bare bones" policy to minimize compliance issues. Other institutions prefer a detailed policy, including procedures, to more clearly communicate the responsibilities of investment personnel. Management must decide on a policy documentation balance that is best for its institution.

ILLUSTRATIVE INVESTMENT POLICY

This investment policy is established as an Appendix to the asset/liability policy established by the board of directors of this financial institution. Investment portfolio activities will be conducted within the guidelines of the Office of the Comptroller of the Currency. All securities will be legal investments eligible for purchase under stated regulatory guidelines.

The purpose of the investment portfolio is to:

- Employ excess customer deposits not needed to meet loan demand;
- Provide liquidity to accommodate deposit and loan fluctuations;
- Secure public and trust deposits, and
- Earn the maximum overall return commensurate with the need for liquidity taking into consideration interest rate sensitivity, credit quality, and needs of the core institution.

Investment targets such as total investment securities, the mix of investment products, and the average life of the investment are derived from the asset/liability long range plan that is updated annually. Strategies to achieve these targets will be developed by the investment officer and presented to the investment management committee of the board of directors at least quarterly.

AUTHORIZED INVESTMENTS

Because new investment products are being continuously developed, the following authorized investments are not necessarily all inclusive. Purchases of securities not included on this list are permissible with prior approval of the investment officer and his/her manager, followed by a review of the investment management committee.

U.S. Government Securities

U.S. government obligations and securities directly guaranteed by the federal government, or securities fully escrowed in U.S. government securities may be purchased without limitation, including zero coupon "stripped" securities with maturities of less than ten years.

U.S. Government Agency Securities

Obligations of U.S. government agencies and securities fully guaranteed by U.S. government agencies may be purchased without limitations.

Municipal Securities

Municipal securities may be purchased under the following guidelines:

1. Concentration of any one municipal revenue issuer or general-obligation political subdivision shall not exceed 10 percent of the institution's capital and surplus.

2. Municipal securities purchased with a maturity of ten years or longer must be rated "A" or better by Moody's or Standard & Poor's unless otherwise approved by the investment management committee.

3. General-obligation and revenue bonds outside the institution's primary market area must be rated "A" or better by Moody's or Standard & Poor's unless otherwise approved by the investment management committee.

4. Municipal securities issued within the institution's primary market area must be rated "Baa" or "BBB" or better by Moody's or Standard & Poor's unless otherwise approved by the investment management committee.

5. Nonrated, noninsured, and marketable issues of municipalities may be purchased if credit quality meets the approval of investment management committee.

6. Marketable industrial revenue bonds may be purchased in the portfolio on an exception basis with the approval of the investment management committee.

7. Nonmarketable, industrial revenue issues shall be treated as loans, subject to proper regulatory compliance and serviced by lending personnel and approved by loan administration rather than being handled as investment securities.

Corporate Securities

Corporate issues, eligible preferred stocks, ESOPS and commercial paper may be purchased, provided that:

1. Purchases of corporate issues, eligible preferred stocks, ESOPS and commercial paper have the prior approval of the Investment Management Committee with proper credit review completed prior to purchase and annual financial statements maintained when applicable.

2. Corporate securities rated "A" or better by Moody's or Standard & Poor's are permissible. Federal regulation requires credit analysis for purchases that exceed 5 percent of capital. This credit review will be completed by the investment officer prior to purchase when applicable. Annual financial statements will be maintained in our files.

3. Investment in any one issuer or obligor shall not exceed 10 percent of the institution's capital and surplus. Total exposure to any one issuer or obligor (including investments, outstanding loans, and commitments) shall not exceed the institution's legal lending limit.

Mortgage Securities

Mortgage-backed securities (MBS or mortgage securities) and their derivatives (Collateralized Mortgage Obligations and Real Estate Mortgage Investment Conduits, hereinafter called CMOs) may be purchased subject to the guidelines and objectives described below.

Overall Exposure

Investments in mortgage securities will be managed so that the overall exposure of the Institution to the mortgage market (including mortgage loans but excluding trading account securities and the mortgage company pipeline) does not exceed four times Tier I capital. Mortgage securities will be managed to achieve diversity in terms of geography, coupon, issuer and prepayments.

Approved Issuers

Approved mortgage securities issuers include the following:

1. GNMA—Government National Mortgage Association.
2. FHLMC—Federal Home Loan Mortgage Association.
3. FNMA—Federal National Mortgage Association.
4. Special Purpose Issuance Subsidiaries—These bankruptcy-remote entities are created to facilitate the issuance of MBS and CMOs. All securities issued by such subsidiaries must be rated in any category of Aa/AA or better and be collateralized by one of the acceptable collateral types.

Approved Collateral

Approved mortgage securities collateral includes the following:

1. Veteran's Administration (VA) or Federal Housing Administration (FHA) loans collateralizing GNMA or FNMA MBS.
2. Loans conforming to FHLMC and FNMA underwriting standards.
3. Collateral of non-conforming, non-securitized loans are acceptable with prior approval of Loan Administration.

Approved Types

Following are approved types of mortgage securities:

1. Fixed rate MBS and derivative products (non-high-risk) and adjustable rate MBS and CMOs issued by GNMA, FHLMC, FNMA, or collateralized by MBS issued by these agencies.
2. Adjustable rate MBS and CMOs, as noted above, are permissible instruments within the scope of this policy.

However, holdings of such floating rate securities should be limited to those market-related indices having correlation to the cost of financial institutions liabilities. The following indices are considered to meet these qualifications:

   a. LIBOR (London Interbank Offer Rate).
   b. Treasury Bill and Note indices.
   c. Prime rate.
   d. 11th District Cost of Funds Index (represents average cost of funds for all thrift institutions in the 11th Federal Home Loan Bank District).
   e. Commercial paper.
   f. Federal funds.
   g. Affiliate bank or composite CD rate.

3. Fixed-rate MBS and derivative products (non-high-risk) and floating-rate MBS and CMOs collateralized by nonconforming nonsecuritized loans with prior approval of Loan Administration.

High-risk Mortgage Securities

In general, any mortgage derivative product that exhibits greater price volatility than a benchmark fixed-rate thirty-year mortgage security will be deemed to be "high risk." For purposes of this policy, a "high-risk" mortgage security is defined as any fixed-rate mortgage derivative product that, at the time of purchase, or at a subsequent testing date, exceeds any of the following tests:

1. Average Life Test—The mortgage derivative product has an expected weighted average life of greater than 10.0 years.

2. Average Life Sensitivity Test—The expected weighted average life of the mortgage derivative product:
   a. Extends by more than 4.0 years, assuming an immediate and sustained parallel shift in the yield curve of plus 300 basis points, or
   b. Shortens by more than 6.0 years, assuming an immediate and sustained parallel shift in the yield curve of minus 300 basis points.

3. Price Sensitivity Test—The estimated change in the price of the mortgage derivative product is more than 17 percent, due to an immediate and sustained parallel shift in the yield curve of plus or minus 300 basis points.

Tests for high-risk securities must be performed both at the purchase date and annually thereafter using consensus prepayment assumptions.

CLASSIFICATION OF INVESTMENT SECURITIES

Investments must be classified in accordance with generally accepted accounting principles (GAAP), and consistent with management's intent to report investments as *held-to-maturity, trading,* or *available-for-sale*. The classification of securities into these categories is made at the time of acquisition, and the appropriateness of the classification must be reviewed at each reporting date.

Held-to-Maturity Securities

This category consists of securities purchased with the positive intent and ability to hold to maturity. These securities are carried at cost, adjusted for amortization of premiums and accretion of discounts.

The objectives of this account are to:
- Meet the investment needs of the core institution;
- Provide securities for pledging to secure certain deposits; and
- Provide assets, which generate an interest income stream for future years.

The institution shall not report securities as held-to-maturity if, in response to certain developments, securities would be considered available-for-sale. Such developments would include, but are not limited to the following:

- Changes in market interest rates or prepayments;
- Need for liquidity;
- Changes in availability of and yield on alternative investments;
- Changes in funding sources and terms; and
- Changes in foreign currency risk.

The sale or transfer of held-to-maturity securities due to certain changes in circumstances shall not be considered to be inconsistent with management's original intent or objective. Under the following circumstances the institution may sell securities in the portfolio and not call into question the classification of other held-to-maturity securities:

- Significant deterioration in the issuer's credit worthiness;
- Change in tax laws (but not a change in tax rate) modifying tax benefits of investments;
- Major business combination or disposition affecting interest rate or credit risk;
- Change in regulations regarding permissible investments;
- Significant increase in capital or risk weights required by regulators;
- Close to maturity or call (within three months); or
- Securities that have received a substantial portion of prepayments of principal (minimum of 85 percent).

Trading Account Securities

The objective of the trading account is to generate earnings through short-term gains on the purchase and sale of securities.

Trading account securities are reported at fair market value, with unrealized gains and losses included in earnings. Limitations as to the amount of risk permissible in the trading account will be established by the investment management committee and reported to the board of directors.

All authorized investment securities may be purchased in the trading account. In addition, the following investments, not prudent for purchase in the held-to-maturity or available-for-sale accounts, may be purchased in the trading account within prescribed trading limits.

- Stripped mortgage-backed securities. (IO—an interest only strip where the investor receives all of the interest cash flows and none of the principal; PO—a principal only strip where the investor receives all of the principal cash flows and none of the interest.)
- All mortgage derivative products considered to be "high-risk" mortgage securities.
- Residuals. (Claims on any excess cash flow from a CMO issue.)
- Zero Coupon Bonds (U.S. Treasury backed with a maturity beyond 10 years.)

Available-for-Sale Securities

The objective of available-for-sale investments is to actively manage assets to maximize net interest income, given interest rate risk requirements established by the Investment Management Committee. This category includes securities purchased without the positive intent and/or ability to hold to maturity.

These securities will be reported at fair market value on a monthly basis, with unrealized gains and losses reported as a separate component of shareholders' equity.

TRANSFER BETWEEN CATEGORIES OF INVESTMENTS

In accordance with FASB Statement 115, transfers between investment categories are to be rare. Transfers from the held-to-maturity category can be made only after proper approval by the investment management committee. This review should include the following considerations:

- Impact on earnings and/or capital;
- Measurement of portfolio's price sensitivity; and
- Past portfolio activity (transfers or sales).

All transfers require the approval of the investment management committee and written explanation detailing appropriate reasons for the transfer.

Transfer of securities between categories of investments shall be accounted for at fair market value. At the date of transfer, any unrealized gain or loss should be accounted for in accordance with the guidelines set forth in FASB Statement 115.

UNSUITABLE INVESTMENT PRACTICES

The following investment practices are not deemed appropriate in the held-to-maturity or available-for-sale accounts but are acceptable in the trading account:

1. Gains trading involves the purchase of a security in the held-to-maturity or available-for-sale categories and the subsequent sale of that same security at a profit after a short-term holding period.

2. When-issued securities trading is the buying and selling of a security during the period between the announcement date and the settlement date of the security.

> *"Transfer of securities between categories of investments shall be accounted for at fair market value."*

3. Pairing-off is a security purchase transaction or other contractual commitment that is closed out or sold at or prior to settlement date or expiration date.

4. Corporate or extended settlement for the purpose of facilitating speculation is considered a trading activity.

5. Short selling that involves the delivery of a security sold short by borrowing it from the investment portfolio is acceptable in the trading account.

6. Covered call option is a strategy that, for a fee, grants the buyer of a call option the right to purchase a security owned by the option writer at a predetermined price before a specified future date.

The following practices are unsuitable in any portfolio account:

1. Adjusted trading is a practice involving the sale of a security to a broker at a price above the prevailing market value and the simultaneous purchase and booking of a different security at a price greater than its market value.

2. Repositioning repurchase agreements, which are used to fund the purchase of securities acquired to resell at a profit or prior to settlement or after a short-term holding period.

3. Delegation of discretionary investment authority to an individual who is not a an employee of the institution or one of its affiliates or to a nonaffiliated firm.

SELECTION OF SECURITY DEALERS

Purchases and sales of securities will be handled with approved broker/dealers. The institution should be familiar with and have reasonable knowledge about the reputation of both the individual broker and his or her firm.

The Institution shall maintain a list of acceptable securities firms and dealers. These firms and dealers shall be subject to an annual review by the investment management committee to determine the ability of the dealer and its subsidiaries or affiliates to fulfill commitments as evidenced by capital strength, liquidity, and operating results. In addition, the dealer or firm's general reputation for financial stability and fair and honest dealings with customers will be considered. The board of directors will approve suggested dealers and firms on an annual basis.

From time to time it might be advantageous to purchase securities from a dealer that is not pre-approved. For example, it is not possible to review the financial statements of all municipal dealers that could own bank qualified securities. In cases where the dealer has not been pre-approved by the board of directors, purchases may be made with the prior approval of the investment management committee and/or president.

DUTIES AND RESPONSIBILITIES

Following are descriptions of the duties and responsibilities of the investment officer and the investment management committee.

Investment Officer

The investment officer is responsible for developing investment strategies for review and approval by the investment management committee. Quarterly, the investment officer shall meet with the investment management committee to recommend investment strategies to accomplish the goals and objectives of the investment portfolio given constraints of liquidity, earnings, and interest rate risk management. Upon approval, the investment officer shall execute these strategies. Further responsibilities include:

- Maintain trade confirmations and other detailed records to support cost basis for all investment purchases and sales;
- Prepare investment trade documentation (see attached) for each security purchase, sale or transfer;
- Satisfy tax and regulatory documentation requirements for bond records and credit files; and
- Prepare all required reports for ALCO, board of directors, and regulatory authorities.

Investment Management Committee

The investment management committee is a committee of the board of directors which shall meet quarterly. The committee is responsible for the overall management and policy implementation of the investment portfolio. The committee's duties are as follows:

- Periodically update investment policy as needed in response to accounting and regulatory promulgations;
- Develop ongoing strategies that guide the use of securities in various categories (*held-to-maturity, trading* and *avail-*

"From time to time it might be advantageous to purchase securities from a dealer that is not pre-approved."

able-for-sale) for the management of interest rate risk, earnings, and capital volatility;

- Review at each reporting date appropriateness of classification of securities;
- Monitor compliance with statutory regulations as well as the institution's investment policy;
- Advance approval of any sale or transfer of securities in the *held-to-maturity* category; and
- Oversee activities of investment officer.

INVESTMENT TRADE DOCUMENTATION

ROA Financial Institution

INVESTMENT TRADE DOCUMENTATION

☐ PURCHASE ☐ SALE ☐ TRANSFER_____

Investment Officer:_____ Trade Date:_____

BROKER: Fed Funds Rate:_____

Par Value (1,000)   Description   Coupon   Mat. Date   Yield   Price   Settlement Date

☐ *Held-to-Maturity*   ☐ *Trading*   ☐ *Available-for-Sale*

| Yld Curve |
| 2 Yr_____ |
| 5 Yr_____ |
| 10 Yr_____ |
| 30 Yr_____ |

Purpose:_____
_____
_____

Special Instructions:_____
_____

AUTHORIZATION:

_____ _____ _____ _____
Investment Officer   Date   Member of Mgmt Investment Committee   Date

Chapter 8: Conclusion and Future of Mark-to-Market

Table of Contents—

Executive Summary
The Future of Mark-to-Market

EXECUTIVE SUMMARY

The advent of Statement 115 marks the beginning of a new era in investment portfolio management. Decisions made now with respect to managing the portfolio will have a long term impact on investment income, liquidity, and control of interest rate risk. Institutions must guard against unnecessarily restricting future investment activities and interest rate risk.

Institutions should not underestimate the difficulty of managing the investment portfolio under Statement 115. Never before has the investment manager had to juggle so many requirements to successfully manage the portfolio. The investment manager must purchase the right bond, at the right time, for the right purpose, at the right price, and place it in the right category. Institutions must remember that they have the burden of proof to justify assumptions and document the classification of investments with sound logic and a track record of compliance. Institutions that are ill-prepared to implement Statement 115 will have a more difficult time defending their plans for managing the investment portfolio.

Statement 115 provides management with a timely opportunity to upgrade the investment planning process. Institutions should perform a comprehensive asset/liability management evaluation to assess interest rate risk and liquidity needs of the investment portfolio in general and the available-for-sale category in particular. Solving the Statement 115 investment classification riddle is not simple. It seems that the best solution is like choosing between the lesser of two evils, a series of compromises. Classifying the investment portfolio involves a risk/reward trade-off. Classifying too many securities as available-for-sale could result in too much capital risk. Classifying too few securities as available-for-sale decreases the liquidity of the investment portfolio.

Most institutions will choose a risk/reward compromise and classify somewhere between one-third and two-thirds of their investments as available-for-sale. Institutions that classify more than two-thirds or less than one-third of the investment portfolio as available-for-sale must support their risk/reward investment decision with appropriate documentation and analysis.

After an institution has determined the approximate size of the available-for sale category, the process of choosing individual securities for this category becomes somewhat easier. Institutions should evaluate "what if" scenarios to choose the best securities for the available-for-sale category given liquidity and capital risk requirements. The decision of how an institution will manage the available-for-sale category will affect the classification of the investment portfolio.

There are two opposing investment management philosophies—total return and buy-and-hold. Some institutions will continue to use a buy-and-hold investment management philosophy, which is a strategy of holding a properly structured investment portfolio to maturity without attempting to "outperform" other investors by finding "cheap" securities or trading the portfolio. Other institutions will use a total return investment management philosophy, believing they can outperform buy-and-hold investors through superior market forecasting or superior ability to find cheap securities through analytics and trading the portfolio. Implied forward rates and horizon analysis are used by investors to enhance total return.

The increased use of derivative instruments is expected to continue as more institutions use these financial engineering tools to manage interest rate risk. The arrival of the mark-to-market era, where institutions seek to protect the investment portfolio from erosion in market value, will only hasten the use of these tools. Institutions must use caution to protect themselves against large losses resulting from counterparty failures or from adverse movements in market rates. Derivative products have become such useful tools to reduce interest rate risk that there is a growing belief among portfolio managers that the failure to use such products is speculative.

THE FUTURE OF MARK-TO-MARKET

If you think Statement 115 was difficult to implement, wait until you see mark-to-market for the rest of the balance sheet. Mark-to-market for investments was relatively easy because investment market values are readily available in an active secondary market.

The difficult part about investments is the classification, not the calculation.

What are deposits worth? Institutions have been trying to answer this question for years and have found no clear answers. Recent deposit outflows into mutual funds suggest fundamental problems with the ability of the banking system to retain core deposits and give rise to questions as to customer loyalty. The cost of bricks and mortar of the branch system compared to the technology of telephonic and other alternative banking delivery methods suggest further questions on the value of customer deposits. How would these mark-to-market issues affect the valuation of deposits?

Clearly, valuation and pricing issues will be the challenge of future mark-to-market endeavors. What are loans worth? Derivatives? Branch systems? Loan and deposit computer software? Where do the questions stop?

Cost-basis accounting worked for the investment portfolio for over half of a century. Now we will try market value accounting for the investment portfolio. There are no magic solutions for investment mark-to-market, just hard work. With the lowest interest rates in 20 to 30 years, perhaps the caution resulting from Statement 115 will be a healthy new beginning to managing the investment portfolio.

Appendix A: Excerpts from An Examiner's Guide to Investments Products and Practices

Off-balance Sheet Products

This section describes the primary off-balance sheet products used by commercial banks; namely, options, swaps, futures, and forwards. The information is designed to identify the products, provide definitions, and aid examiners in evaluating bank management's proficiency in using the products. This section focuses on a purchasing bank's use of the products, but sometimes refers to dealer operations to clarify and provide more comprehensive background information.

Since managing financial risk is becoming more important to banks, the use of off-balance sheet products will continue to grow. As the markets become more liquid and information is proliferated, more banks will use off-balance sheet products to manage various risks or to improve income through speculating on price movements. Examiners must understand the characteristics of these products and the techniques for managing the risks they create.

Options

I. Product Description

The owner of an option contract has the right to buy or sell a specified asset, at a specified price, on or before a specified date. The party granting the right is referred to as the option seller, or writer, and the party receiving the option is called the option buyer. The seller is obligated to perform on the contract, whereas the purchaser has a right, but not an obligation, to perform on the contract.

A call option gives the buyer the right to purchase the underlying instrument and a put option gives the buyer the right to sell the underlying instrument. Purchasing a call option is considered a long position and the buyer expects to profit from the price of the underlying instrument exceeding the strike, or exercise price, within the life of the contract. The put purchaser expects to profit from the price of the underlying instrument declining below the exercise price of the contract. The exercise price is the price at which the contract owner has the right to buy or sell the underlying instrument. Return profiles of a long call, a long put, a short call, and a short put are shown in the facing column.

Options are available on a myriad of instruments. However, commercial banks typically use interest rate and currency options. These types of options can be used in bank dealer activities, in a trading account, or to hedge various risks associated with the underlying instruments or portfolio. This discussion will be limited to the uses of purchased instruments, rather than the trading or warehousing of products.

Interest Rate Options

Interest rate options are available on several different contracts, indices, and futures contracts traded on various exchanges. The presence of an exchange offers liquidity to the market and reduces credit risk because the exchange stands between all trades. Banks are permitted to engage in these contracts to manage overall interest rate exposure, exposure on a specific contract, or in conjunction with the trading department.

Options on short-term interest rates are available on the Chicago Board Options Exchange (CBOE). These options are on the 13-week T-bill rate, which is the recognized benchmark for short-term interest

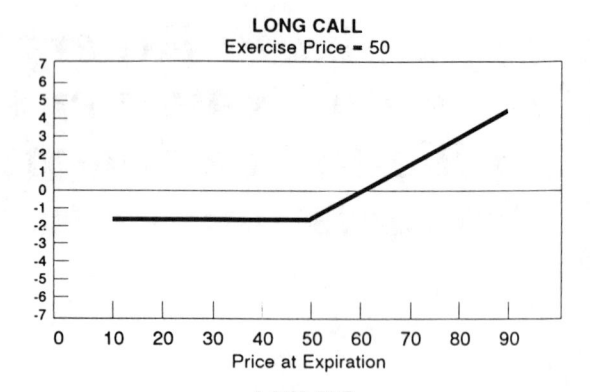

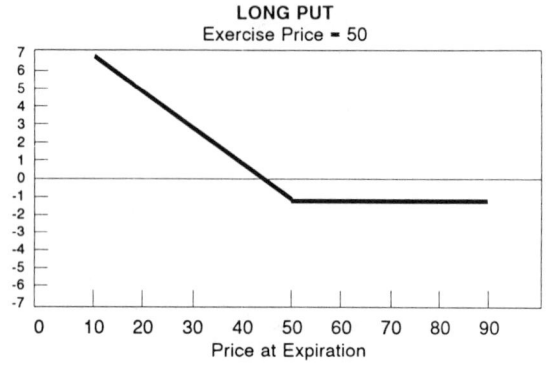

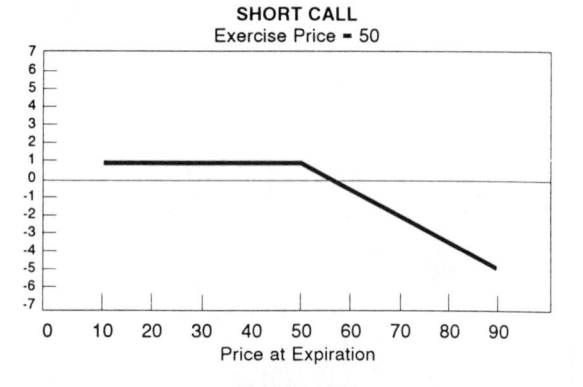

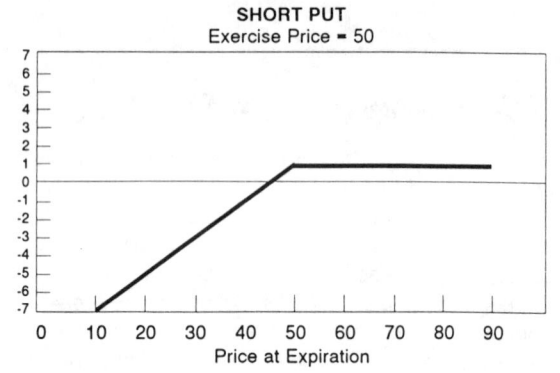

82

124 Appendix A

rates. Other short-term interest rate options include options on Eurodollar time deposit futures contracts and those on T-bill futures contracts. These instruments are available on the International Monetary Market (IMM) of the Chicago Mercantile Exchange.

Options on long-term interest rates are also available on the CBOE. These options are based on the average yield to maturity of the 7- and 10-year T-notes and the 30-year T-bond. Other long- and intermediate-term interest rate options include options on T-bonds and T-notes and are available on the Chicago Board of Trade (CBOT).

Interest rate options are also available in the OTC market. OTC interest rate options are used by banks because they can be specially tailored to fit a bank's particular risk management needs. They are not standardized like the exchange traded options and can have as long a maturity as required to hedge the particular interest rate risk. The OTC options used primarily by banks are interest rate caps, floors, and collars.

An interest rate cap, or ceiling, allows a party to hedge against increasing interest rates over a predetermined rate for a specified period of time. The purchaser of an interest rate cap receives from the cap writer the excess of a reference rate (usually a floating rate index), over the cap rate. The payment received, if any, will occur on specified settlement dates. If the cap rate equals or exceeds the reference rate, no payments are made. An example of when management would purchase an interest rate cap would be if the bank were liability sensitive, when asset repricing maturities were longer than their liability repricings, and management decided that the probability of rates increasing was high. An interest rate cap could be purchased, and if rates increased as expected, the profit on the interest rate cap could be used to offset the bank's increased funding costs.

An interest rate floor allows the purchaser to hedge against rates declining below a specified (floor) rate over a period of time. The purchaser of the floor will receive payments from the floor writer when the reference rate falls below the floor rate. The payments will be the difference between the floor rate and the reference rate. If the floor rate is less than the reference rate, no payments are made. An example of when management would purchase an interest rate floor would be if the bank were asset sensitive, where asset repricing maturities were shorter than liability repricings, and management decided that the probability of rates declining was high. An interest rate floor could be purchased and if rates did decrease as expected, the profit on the floor could be used to offset lower yields on the variable rate assets.

An interest rate collar is a combination of a cap and a floor. The purchaser of a collar buys a cap and sells a floor. The premium earned on the floor offsets the price paid for the cap. The collar essentially allows the bank to receive cap protection at a reduced premium cost. However, the bank sacrifices the right to fully benefit from a substantial drop in rates since the collar only allows the bank to benefit from falling rates until the floor is reached.

Currency Options

Currency option trading is a large part of many large banks' trading operations. These options are traded for customers, traded for profit, and used in the overall management of exposure to foreign exchange. Exchange traded options are available on all major currencies, including the U.S. Dollar, Japanese Yen, German Deutschemark, British Pound Sterling, Swiss Franc, Canadian Dollar, French Franc and Australian Dollar. Options on the futures contracts of these "major" currencies are also traded on various exchanges. Options on several other currencies are available on various exchanges. The most liquid of the currencies are the Mark, Yen, Pound, and $US.

Currency options can be used to hedge a bank's exposure to foreign exchange rate movements. This exposure can come from various sources, including loans and securities denominated in foreign currencies. An example of when a bank would use a foreign currency option would be if it had a bond denominated in German Marks. If the mark depreciates against the dollar while the bank holds the bond, the bank will lose money when converting the marks back to dollars. Bank management could purchase a put option on the mark which allows the bank to sell the mark at a given price. If the mark does depreciate, the profit on the put could be used to offset the exchange loss on the mark-denominated bond.

II. Market—Where to Find Current Value and Ratings

Options contracts can be exchange traded, standardized, and traded on an organized exchange, or over-the-counter (OTC), which are customized and usually to accommodate a specialized hedging requirement. Exchange-traded options are traded on several exchanges, both in the U.S. and abroad. Exchange-traded options have standardized specifications and the exchange is the counterparty on all trades, thus reducing credit risk. The counterparty on an OTC option can be a broker-dealer, institution, or an individual. Therefore, OTC options usually contain more credit risk, along with the other risks associated with exchange-traded options. The "Money and Investing" section of *The Wall Street Journal* contains price information on exchange-traded options traded in the U.S.

III. What You Should Look for (Suitability)

Options are legitimate products that commercial banks may use to hedge various interest rate and currency risks. The most obvious approach would be hedging a specific instrument with a specific option. For example, management has a T-bond that it wants to hedge to counter a rise in interest rates, which would cause the price of its bond to drop. Management could purchase a put on the T-bond giving it the right to put the bond to the option seller at a pre-determined price. If rates rise, the bank can put the bond and avoid a loss. If rates do not rise, management has only lost the money paid for the option.

Options strategies can also be used to enhance returns on specific instruments or on a portfolio of instruments. An example of this would be covered call writing. The premium received on the call option will enhance the overall return on the bond. Management must consider, however, that if the price of the bond rises, it risks having the bond called away. Banks that write covered call options must report the underlying security as held for sale at the lower of cost or market value. However, if the bank chooses to continue to carry the underlying security at amortized cost, its policies and procedures must prohibit the delivery of the underlying security. A written agreement with the option holder must state that the bank will settle only in cash upon exercise of the option.

Options can also be used to speculate on price movements. This activity should be limited to banks with strong capital and the management sophistication to manage the risks involved. Management must be able to explain the reasons for their options strategies. The line between hedging and speculating is often thin.

The examiner must ensure that bank management understands the risks associated with these products and implements systems and controls to quantify and manage those risks. Specifically, this will include an analysis of the following:

Policies: Management must implement specific written policies which authorize the activities in which the bank will engage. The policies should set limits for all the risks associated with these products including, but not limited to, position limits, maturity limits, credit limits, and earnings-at-risk limits. These limits should be incorporated into the risk management system used by the bank. Limits should also be established for delta, gamma, vega, and theta (refer to the paragraph on Other Risk in this section).

Procedures: Management must establish procedures and internal controls to ensure that policy limits are enforced. Procedures should be written for credit approval; segregation of duties in operations; revaluation, if necessary; and, provision of periodic reports to management.

Risk Management System: The risk management system must include a model to quantify accurately the risk associated with the position and to provide the means to manage the risk effectively. The risk should be monitored relative to the limits imposed by the policies. In hedging situations, correlation studies for the appropriate instruments should detail the mechanics of the hedge. Examiners must ensure the accuracy of the models used to measure and monitor the risk. This may include analyzing earnings of the position, or the gains and losses associated with given hedges, and comparing these to the expected result. The system must incorporate all risks associated with the product and accurately reflect them relative to limits on earnings at risk.

Audit: Internal and external audits should be performed on this area. Examiners must determine the adequacy of each. This should focus particularly on the effectiveness of internal controls and the adequacy of the management information system. This area should also address management's willingness to implement the proper control systems to monitor activities of this sophistication. Examiners will also determine the expertise of the auditors.

The lack of the above information may lead to unsafe and unsound banking practices.

IV. Accounting Treatment

A bank engaging in options should have accounting policies and procedures that include recordkeeping requirements, and methods for determining whether options are reducing or increasing risk and for accounting for each option, based on its type and purpose. Accounting policies and procedures for options should be approved by the board of directors. They should be designed to ensure consistent and appropriate accounting for options.

Regulatory accounting requirements for options are in the Call Report. The accounting method used depends on whether the bank has sold (written) or purchased the option.

Accounting by the Purchaser

The purchaser of an option does not record market valuation adjustments. If the market value of the underlying financial instrument is unfavorable relative to the contract price, the purchaser will generally allow the option to expire unexercised. The purchaser recognizes a gain only at the time the option is exercised.

The par value of the instruments underlying each outstanding option contract purchased should be reported in Call Report Schedule RC-L "Off-Balance Sheet Items." The notional principal amount of caps, floors, and collars is also included in Schedule RC-L of the Call Report.

For all options contracts, netting of purchased options against written options is not permitted. In addition, banks may not offset their written options to buy against their written options to sell.

Accounting by the Seller

The seller of an option must account for that option at the lower of its cost or market value. In addition, fee income received by the seller of an option must be deferred until the option expires, is exercised, or is terminated. Market values of outstanding written options should be determined at least monthly and more often if the bank maintains a material amount of these contracts.

The determination of the lower of cost or market adjustment depends on whether the seller of the option is obligated to purchase or sell the underlying asset. If the seller of the option is obligated to *purchase* the underlying asset, losses are recorded if the market value of the asset is less than the contract price minus the deferred option fee. For example, assume the bank wrote an option to purchase a Treasury note in 30 days for $100,000. The bank received a fee of $1,000 for a net contract price of $99,000. If the current market value of the Treasury note is $98,000, the bank would record an unrealized loss of $1,000.

If the seller of the option is obligated to *sell* the underlying asset, losses are recorded if the market value of the underlying asset is greater than the contract price plus the deferred option fee. For example, assume the bank wrote an option to sell a Treasury note in 30 days for $100,000. The bank received a fee of $1,000 for a net contract price of $101,000. If the current market value of the Treasury note is $102,000, the bank would record an unrealized loss of $1,000.

Unrealized losses are reported as other noninterest expense in the Call Report with an offsetting entry to other liabilities. If there is no unrealized loss, deferred fees are recorded as other liabilities. If an option contract expires unexercised, any related deferred fee income may be reported as other income.

If an option contract is settled prior to its maturity, the deferred fee income is accounted for as an adjustment of the settlement amount. Net settlement gains are reported as other noninterest income. Net settlement expenses are reported as other noninterest expense.

If an option requires the seller to purchase an asset, the deferred fee income is used to reduce the cost basis of the acquired asset if the option is exercised. Assets acquired should be recorded at the lower of this adjusted cost or their market value on the date of purchase. If an option requires the seller to sell an asset, the deferred fee income should be accounted for as an increase in the sales price of the asset sold.

V. Risks

Interest Rate Risk: Only open positions will possess interest rate risk. Using an option as a hedging vehicle is intended to reduce interest rate risk.

Credit Risk: Negligible for exchange-traded options because the exchange is the counter party on every trade. OTC options contain credit risk because the purchaser (and not the seller) is exposed to the counterparty performing on the contract. The exposure is limited to the amount of the cost to maintain the required position if the counterparty fails to perform. Also, credit risk is only evident if the option is in-the-money. There is no risk if the option is out-of-the-money because it will go unexercised.

Liquidity Risk: Liquidity risk depends on the contract and the expiration. Usually, OTC contracts contain more liquidity risk since they are customized contracts that may serve only a specified purpose.

Other Risk: Theoretical risk measures.

Delta measures the sensitivity of an option's price for a given change in the spot price of the underlying commodity.

Gamma measures the sensitivity of Delta to changes in the price of the underlying instrument. It measures the amount Delta will move when the spot rate moves. It is very important when hedging because it determines the amount the option book will have to change to maintain an effective hedge.

Theta, or time decay, is the sensitivity of an option's price to the passage of time. The value of an option will decrease as time passes, but it does not do so at an even rate. Theta can also be thought of as "rent" paid for maintaining a gamma position.

Vega, or volatility risk, is the sensitivity of the price of an option to changes in volatility.

VI. Legal Limitations

Options are not considered investment securities under 12 U.S.C. 24(7th). However, the use of these contracts is considered to be an activity incidental to banking, within safe and sound banking principles. Refer to subsection III, Suitability, in this section for details on the systems, controls and limits which bank management must implement prior to engaging in options activities.

VII. Risk-based Capital Requirement

Foreign exchange, commodity, and interest rate contracts have the following process for determining the risk-based capital requirement. Three steps determine: the current credit exposure; the potential credit exposure; and the risk-weight. Additional details follow:

1. Mark to market (positive values only).

2. Add-on for potential credit exposure:

   — Interest Rate 0 % ($\leq$ 1 Yr.) .5 % (> 1 Yr.)
   — Exchange Rate 1 % ($\leq$ 1 Yr.) 5 % (> 1 Yr.)

3. Assign to Risk Category,
   Maximum 50 percent.

The risk-based capital requirement is computed by multiplying the sum of the current and potential credit exposure (step one plus step two) *by* the risk weight (step three).

Note also that exchange rate contracts that have an original maturity of 14 calendar days or less and instruments traded on exchanges and subject to daily margin requirements are *exempt* from the risk-based capital calculation.

(Further details relative to the risk-based capital calculation can be found in the *Comptroller's Manual for National Banks* under 12 CFR 3.1, Appendix A. If the regulation is still not clear, the Chief National Bank Examiner's Office can assist in finding an answer.)

III. References

Fabozzi, Frank J., ed., *The Handbook of Fixed Income Securities*, 2d ed. (Homewood, Illinois: Dow Jones-Irwin, 1987).

McMillan, Lawrence G., *Options as a Strategic Investment*, 2d ed. (New York: New York Institute of Finance, 1986).

Oberhofer, George D., *Rate Risk Management: Fixed Income Strategies Using Futures, Options and Swaps* (Chicago: Probus Publishing Company, 1988).

Siegel, Daniel R., and Diane F. Siegel, *The Futures Markets: Arbitrage, Risk Management and Portfolio Strategies* (Chicago: Probus Publishing Company, 1990).

Smith, Jr., Clifford W., Charles W. Smithson, and D. Sykes Wilford, *Managing Financial Risk* (New York: HarperCollins, 1990).

OCC Documents

Bank Accounting Advisory Series, Issue No. 1, June 1990.

Comptroller's Handbook for National Bank Examiners, Section 203 (Washington, D.C., March 1990).

Banking Circular 79 (3rd Rev.), National Bank Participation in the Financial Futures and Forward Placement Markets, April 19, 1983.

Swaps

I. Product Description

A swap is a contract between two counterparties to exchange net cash flows on agreed upon dates, for a specified period of time, on an established notional principal. The payment to one or the other counterparties is the difference between the two cash flows. The contracts are usually done between a swap dealer and a customer, rather than between two customers. The swap market originated in the foreign exchange markets in the early 1970s and has since spread to interest rates and commodities. Banks use interest rate swaps as an asset/liability tool to hedge undesired mismatches. The notional principal outstanding of interest rate swaps has grown to well over $1 trillion. The commodity swap market is relatively new to domestic banks and is continuing to evolve. The basic structure of a swap is shown below. The example uses a fixed for floating interest rate swap, but the basic structure and mechanics are similar for all swaps.

Although swaps are over-the-counter instruments, meaning they are not traded on an organized exchange, there is a degree of standardization in the contracts since the advent of International Swap Dealers Association (ISDA). Counterparties often form a master swap agreement that establishes the basic language of a swap agreement. Master agreements often incorporate the *ISDA Code of Standard Wording, Assumptions, and Provisions for Swaps* to provide basic wording and assumptions. Counterparties can change the master agreement as required.

Banks are a natural intermediary in the swap markets because they, and their customers, have exposure to interest rate, currency and commodity price movements. Banks can offer swaps as a risk management tool for their customers. Also, since banks are in the business of evaluating credit risk, they are suited to analyze their customers' credit risk with the bank itself. Customers do not have to find a

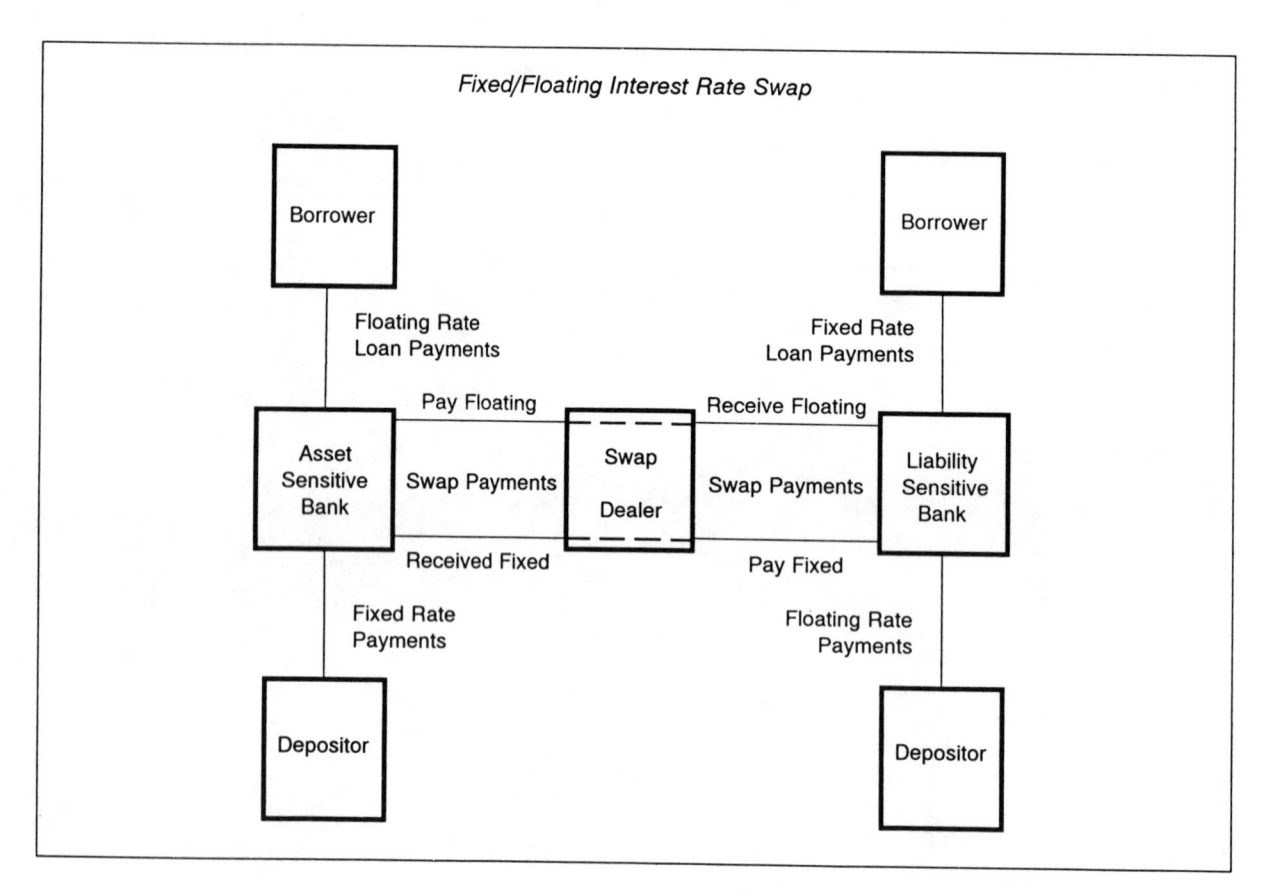

Fixed/Floating Interest Rate Swap

counterparty for their transaction or analyze the counterparty's credit quality.

Banks can run a book of swaps and manage the overall risk on a portfolio basis rather than on a contract-by-contract basis, which is virtually impossible because of the inherently unmatched nature of the swap market.

Currency Swaps

Currency swaps, the oldest type of swap, originated as multinational companies began experiencing increased foreign exchange risk after the breakdown of the Bretton Woods fixed exchange rate system in 1973. A currency swap is similar to an interest rate swap, except the cash flows are based on two different fixed currency rates (e.g., fixed dollar rate for a fixed yen rate).

Interest Rate Swaps

Banks generally will use interest rate swaps in two ways. The first way is as an end user in the overall asset/lability and interest rate risk programs. The swaps will be used to lower their cost of funds or to manage exposure to interest rate movements. The second use normally seen in banks will be as a dealer in the swap market. Several large banks are market makers in interest rate swaps and act as principal for their customers. This type of operation is usually found in the trading or capital markets division of a bank.

Interest rate swaps can be broken into coupon swaps and basis swaps. A coupon swap exchanges an interest payment stream of one configuration for another on the same notional principal, e.g., fixed rate for floating rate. A basis swap bases payments on two floating rate indices, e.g., LIBOR for Prime. Interest rate swaps are also used to lower a bank's cost of funds by exploiting credit spreads between the fixed and floating rate markets.

Commodity Swaps

On July 17, 1989, the Commodity Futures Trading Commission (CFTC) gave banks broad exemption from regulation relative to swap transactions involving commodities. A commodity swap is a financial contract between two counterparties that has a periodic payout over its life equal to the net difference between a fixed price and the currently prevailing spot price for a given volume of a commodity. The swap allows an entity to hedge income or expense structures that are sensitive to the price volatility of one or more commodities.

Since the CFTC exemption, bank participation in this market has been growing rapidly. The majority of the business has been in petroleum products, specifically crude oil and heating oil. The business escalated after the crisis in the Persian Gulf surfaced in August 1990. However, banks have begun to deal in other energy products, such as jet fuel and natural gas and in various metals. To date, the business has been concentrated in large, sophisticated institutions that have the systems capability and technical expertise to manage the risks associated with this product.

II. Market—Where to Find Current Value and Ratings

Swaps are not exchange traded products and have no easily accessible market prices and ratings. Swap dealers quote prices based on the terms of the swap and prices are quoted on a Reuters screen; however, there is no other easily accessible market data.

III. What You Should Look for (Suitability)

Interest rate, currency, and commodity swaps are legitimate products that banks may use to hedge various risks associated with interest rate, currency, and commodity price movements.

Interest rate swaps generally will be used as an asset/liability management strategy to hedge exposure to fixed or floating rates (coupon swap), to floating rate indices (basis swap), or to lower funding costs. For example, a coupon swap would be used by a bank which has a positive gap (fixed rate funding and floating assets). The bank could enter into a swap agreement with a dealer in which it pays a floating rate and receives a fixed rate, thus achieving a more neutral asset/liability position.

A basis swap could be used if the bank's deposits were tied to the commercial paper rate, while its loans were tied to LIBOR. Although both indices are floating, they do not have 100 percent correlation and could expose the bank to basis risk. The bank could merely enter into a swap in which it receives the commercial paper rate and pays LIBOR, thus limiting its exposure to the basis differentials between LIBOR and the commercial paper rate.

Only banks with sophisticated risk management systems should offer these products as risk management tools for customers (i.e., trading).

The examiner must determine whether bank management understands the risks associated with these products and implements systems and controls to quantify and manage those risks effectively. Specifically, this will include an analysis of the following:

Policies: Management must implement specific written policies that authorize the activities in which the bank will engage. The policies should set limits for all the various risks associated with these products including, but not limited to, position limits, maturity limits, credit limits, and earnings-at-risk limits.

Procedures: Management must establish procedures and internal controls to ensure that policy limits are enforced. Procedures should be written for credit approval; segregation of duties in operations; revaluation, if necessary; and, provision of periodic reports to management.

Risk Management System: The risk management system must include a model to quantify the risk associated with the position and to provide the means to manage that risk effectively. The risk should be monitored relative to the limits imposed by the policies. In hedging situations, correlation studies for the appropriate instruments should detail the mechanics of the hedge. Examiners must ensure the accuracy of the models used to measure and monitor the risk. This may include analyzing earnings of the position, or the gains and losses associated with given hedges, and comparing them to the expected result. The system must incorporate all risks associated with the product and accurately reflect them relative to limits on earnings at risk.

Audit: Internal and external audits should be performed. Examiners must determine the adequacy of each. This should focus particularly on the effectiveness of internal controls and the adequacy of the management information system. This area should also address management's willingness to implement the proper control systems to monitor activities of this sophistication. Examiners will also determine the expertise of the auditors.

The lack of the above information may lead to unsafe and unsound banking practices.

IV. Accounting Treatment

A bank engaging in swaps should have accounting policies and procedures that include recordkeeping requirements and methods for determining whether swaps are reducing risk or increasing risk and for accounting for each swap, based on its type and purpose. Accounting policies and procedures for swaps should be approved by the board of directors. They should be designed to ensure consistent and appropriate accounting for swaps.

Some banks may recognize interest income using the accrual method, similar to other earning assets of the bank. That is, they will accrue the interest income or expense associated with a swap, based on current rates. The income or expense is then recognized over the life of the swap.

Other banks may adopt a more aggressive approach and "upfront" their swap income for "matched" swap positions. This is done by recording, at inception, the present value of the total expected net cash flows of the matched swaps. Banks adopting this method generally believe that the swap is a trading account security and the present value of the net cash flows represents the fair market value of the swap position.

To illustrate the difference between the accrual method and the upfronting method, assume a bank enters into a $10 million notional amount interest rate swap to pay a fixed rate of 9.2 percent and receive LIBOR. They also enter into a $10 million notional amount swap to receive a fixed rate of 9.3 percent and pay LIBOR. The term of both swaps is five years. The bank effectively has a built in spread of .1 percent on this position. Under the accrual method, the bank recognizes monthly swap income of $833 (annual spread of .1 percent times $10 million notional amount divided by 12 months). Using the upfronting method, the bank recognizes an immediate gain of approximately $38,000 (the present value of the five-year net cash flows from the swap, assuming a 10 percent discount rate). This $38,000 is then amortized over the life of the swap agreements.

Upfronting swap income raises several concerns. First, the present value calculation is a mechanical process, subject to the assumptions of the bank. Discount rates used to compute this present value are difficult to establish and vary greatly between banks.

Another concern is the fact that significant interest rate, credit, operational, and legal risks remain over the life of the swap. These risks may cause the bank actually to realize less income than previously recognized.

In practice, banks that upfront their swap income rarely have perfectly matched swap contracts. Often, the maturities and notional amounts differ. Transactions involving the upfronting of income should be examined closely to ascertain that the bank has not overstated its income materially.

The notional value of all outstanding interest rate swap and similar agreements should be reported in Schedule RC-L. Netting swap agreements is not permitted for regulatory reporting.

V. Risks

Interest Rate Risk: When a swap is used to hedge existing interest rate risk, the overall risk should be lessened. Unmatched positions will have interest rate or basis risk; however, purchasing banks should not engage in this activity.

Credit Risk: Credit risk exists in the swap market because the counterparty may not fulfill the contract. The credit risk for swaps is greater than that for futures, but less than the amount for forwards (pure credit risk). Also, the swap will have credit risk only when it is in-the-money, and not when it is out of the money. The bank must ensure proper credit analysis and proper credit approval to manage this risk.

Liquidity Risk: Liquidity risk varies with the type of swap. Interest rate and currency swaps have liquid markets, but commodity swaps are relatively new and the liquidity in this market is not as deep.

Other Risk: Settlement Risk: Settlement risk exists on the days when the cash flows are exchanged. Bank management must establish proper settlement limits and procedures to monitor the processing of these limits.

VI. Legal Limitations

Swaps are not considered investment securities under 12 U.S.C. 24(7th). However, the use of these contracts is considered to be an activity incidental to banking, within safe and sound banking principles. (Refer to subsection III, Suitability, in this section for details on the systems, controls and limits that bank management must implement prior to engaging in swap activities.)

VII. Risk-based Capital Requirement

Foreign exchange, commodity, and interest rate contracts have the following process for determining the risk-based capital requirement. Three steps determine: the current credit exposure; the potential credit exposure; and the risk-weight. Additional details follow:

1. Mark to market (positive values only).

2. Add-on for potential credit exposure:

   — Interest Rate 0 % ($\leq$ 1 Yr.) .5 % (> 1 Yr.)
   — Exchange Rate 1 % ($\leq$ 1 Yr.) 5 % (> 1 Yr.)

3. Assign to Risk Category, Maximum 50 percent.

The risk-based capital requirement is computed by multiplying the sum of the current and potential credit exposure (step one plus step two) *by* the risk weight (step three).

Note also that exchange rate contracts that have an original maturity of 14 calendar days or less and instruments traded on exchanges and subject to daily margin requirements are *exempt* from the risk-based capital calculation.

(Further details relative to risk-based capital calculation can be found in the *Comptroller's Manual for National Banks* under 12 CFR 3.1, Appendix A. If the regulation is still not clear, the Chief National Bank Examiner's Office can assist in finding an answer.)

VIII. References

Fabozzi, Frank J., ed., *The Handbook of Fixed Income Securities*, 2d ed. (Homewood, Illinois: Dow Jones-Irwin, 1987).

McMillan, Lawrence G., *Options as a Strategic Investment*, 2d ed. (New York: New York Institute of Finance, 1986).

Oberhofer, George D., *Rate Risk Management: Fixed Income Strategies Using Futures, Options and*

Swaps (Chicago: Probus Publishing Company, 1988).

Siegel, Daniel R., and Diane F. Siegel, *The Futures Markets: Arbitrage, Risk Management and Portfolio Strategies* (Chicago: Probus Publishing Company, 1990).

Smith, Jr., Clifford W., Charles W. Smithson, and D. Sykes Wilford, *Managing Financial Risk* (New York: HarperCollins, 1990).

OCC Documents

Bank Accounting Advisory Series, Issue No. 1, June 1990.

Comptroller's Handbook for National Bank Examiners, Section 203 (Washington, D.C., March 1990).

Futures

I. Product Description

A futures contract is an obligation to deliver or receive a specified amount of a commodity or financial instrument at a specified price on a specific date in the future. No cash is passed between the buyer and seller at the inception of the contract. Also, futures contracts rarely settle by actual delivery of the underlying commodity; instead, they are cash settled. Futures contracts are traded on several exchanges in the U.S. and abroad and are available on several financial instruments and commodities. This section will focus on futures on debt instruments and commodities because they are the contracts primarily used by banks.

Interest rate futures are used to speculate on interest rate movements or to hedge exposure to them. This section will focus on the hedging aspects of interest rate futures, although the line drawn between the hedger and the speculator is often indistinct.

Futures contracts are available on government securities, mortgage-backed securities, and Eurodollar time deposits, all of which can be used to hedge interest rate exposure. Typical uses will be to hedge the risk of a particular security, portfolio of securities, or as an asset/liability tool to hedge overall balance sheet exposure.

Using futures contracts in the ways listed above substitutes basis risk for interest rate risk. Although the interest rate risk may be hedged with the offsetting futures contract, the basis differential between the cash and futures markets must be managed. Bank management must determine the correlation between the cash and futures markets relative to all the hedging arrangements used by the bank.

Currency futures are available on major currencies and can be used to hedge exposure to currency movements. An example would be a bank that purchased a foreign currency denominated bond. In addition to the risks associated with domestic bonds, foreign bonds also have foreign exchange risk. If the currency in which the bond is denominated depreciates against the dollar over the term of the bond, the bank will lose money when the bond is exchanged for dollars. However, if the bank enters into a futures contract to ensure a specific amount (the amount of the bond plus interest), at a specific price, and at a specific time (the maturity date of the bond), the foreign exchange risk can be managed.

Commodity futures will be used primarily to hedge commodity risk incurred from mismatches in swap positions. Since purchasing banks will not be running a commodity swap portfolio, the hedging uses of commodity futures used by commodity swap dealers will not be discussed. The principles are the same as those for interest rate or currency futures.

II. Market—Where to Find Current Value and Ratings

Futures on a variety of underlying instruments are traded on various exchanges around the world. The "Money and Investing" section of *The Wall Street Journal* has the prices of futures contracts traded on domestic exchanges.

III. What You Should Look for (Suitability)

Futures contracts are legitimate risk management products that banks may use to hedge risks associated with interest rate or currency price movements. One of the most common strategies is to hedge a specific instrument with a specific futures contract. For example, a bank owns a $1MM T-bond and management believes interest rates may rise, thus causing the value of this bond to fall. Management could short sell the equivalent of $1MM of T-bond futures (10 $100M contracts). If rates rise and the price of the bond declines, the loss will be offset by the profit associated with the short futures position.

Bank management may also use futures contracts to hedge undesired asset/liability mismatches. For example, a negative gap position could be hedged by shorting interest rate futures. If interest rates rise and cause margins to narrow, the gain associated with the short futures position will offset this loss. Conversely, long positions in interest rate futures contracts could be used to hedge an undesired positive gap. If rates decline, causing the interest sensitive assets to yield less, the gain on the futures position will help offset the loss. Keep in mind that with either of the above two strategies, the amount of futures contracts bought or sold should reflect the amount of interest sensitive assets or liabilities that management desires to hedge.

Speculating in futures should be done only by those banks with strong capital and the level of risk management sophistication necessary to manage this type of activity.

The examiner must ensure that bank management understands the risks associated with these products and implements systems and controls to effectively quantify and manage those risks. Specifically, this will include an analysis of the following:

Policies: Management must implement specific written policies that authorize the activities in which the bank will engage. The policies should set limits for the risks associated with these products including, but not limited to, position limits, maturity limits, credit limits, and earnings-at-risk limits that should be incorporated into the risk management system used by the bank.

Procedures: Management must establish procedures and internal controls to ensure that policy limits are enforced. Procedures should be written for credit approval; segregation of duties in operations; revaluation; and, provision of periodic reports to management.

Risk Management System: The risk management system must include a model to quantify accurately the risk associated with the position and provide the means to effectively manage that risk. The risk should be monitored relative to the limits imposed by the policies. In hedging situations, correlation studies for the appropriate instruments should detail the mechanics of the hedge. Examiners must ensure the accuracy of the models used to measure and monitor the risk. This may include analyzing earnings of the position or the gains and losses associated with given hedges and comparing them to the expected result. The system must incorporate all risks associated with the product and accurately reflect them relative to limits on earnings at risk.

Audit: Internal and external audits should be performed. Examiners must determine the adequacy of each. Audits should particularly focus on the effectiveness of internal controls and the adequacy of management information systems. This area should also address management's willingness to implement the proper control systems to monitor activities of this sophistication. Examiners will also determine the expertise of the auditors.

The lack of the above information may lead to unsafe and unsound banking practices.

IV. Accounting Treatment

A bank engaging in futures should have accounting policies and procedures that include recordkeeping requirements and methods for determining whether futures are reducing risk or increasing risk and for accounting for futures contracts. Accounting policies and procedures for futures should be approved by the board of directors. They should be designed to ensure consistent and appropriate accounting for futures.

Accounting for futures should follow the requirements of the Instructions to the Call Report. The Call Report requires banks to account for futures consistently, either at market value or at the lower of cost or market value.

Market values on all futures should be determined at least monthly, or more often, if the bank has a material amount of these contracts.

The par value of outstanding futures should be reported in Call Report Schedule RC-L "Off-Balance Sheet Items." For reporting purposes, contracts are considered outstanding until they have been cancelled by acquisition or delivery of the underlying security, or, for futures *only*, by offset. For Call Report purposes, offset is defined as the purchase and sale of an equal number of contracts on the same underlying instrument for the same delivery month, executed through the same clearing member on the same exchange.

Offsetting allows a bank to net the contracts involved to report in Schedule RC-L. Note, however, that offsetting is permitted only for futures contracts that meet the above requirements and not for forwards.

For futures that are accounted for on a mark-to-market basis, net valuation gains should be reported as other noninterest income in the Call Report. Net valuation losses should be reported as other noninterest expense. For futures that are accounted for on a lower of cost or market basis, write-downs to market are recorded as other noninterest expense on the Call Report.

Note that regulatory accounting does not permit loss or gain deferral for futures (hedge accounting). In other words, a bank accounts for these contracts the same, whether they are entered into for speculative or hedging purposes. The only exception to this policy is for mortgage banking operations. Banks are permitted to use hedge accounting for mortgage banking operations.

V. Risks

Interest Rate Risk: Varies with the purpose and types of contracts used. Open futures positions will have interest rate risk just as an open position in other types of contracts. Futures contracts should be used to hedge (rather than increase) interest rate risk on a bank-wide basis.

Credit Risk: Virtually no credit risk because the exchange stands between all trades.

Liquidity Risk: Little liquidity risk involved with financial futures. However, open interest and other position limits should be implemented and monitored to ensure that a position does not become too large to unwind at a reasonable price. Furthermore, liquidity risk must be monitored and understood for the various products. Some types of futures have much more liquidity than other futures. Also, liquidity is generally greater for short dated contracts and less as the maturities increase.

Other Risk: Settlement Risk, Basis Risk

Settlement risk will exist when the contract expires and the underlying instrument will be delivered. Settlement limits should be established by contract and by counterparty.

Basis risk exists when using futures contracts as hedges because futures and cash prices do not always move in the same manner. Management needs to address and manage this risk particularly when the contract type or maturity of the two instruments is not exactly matched.

VI. Legal Limitations

Futures are not considered investment securities under 12 U.S.C. 24(7th). However, the use of these contracts is considered to be an activity incidental to banking, within safe and sound banking principles. Refer to subsection III, Suitability, in this section for details on systems, controls, and limits that bank management must implement prior to engaging in futures contract activities.

VII. Risk-based Capital Weight

Futures contracts are exempt from risk-based capital weighting, because they are traded on organized exchanges which require daily margin payments.

(Further details relative to the risk-based capital weighting calculation can be found in the *Comptroller's Manual for National Banks* under 12 CFR 3.1, Appendix A. If the regulation is still not clear, the Chief National Bank Examiner's Office can assist in finding an answer.)

VIII. References

Fabozzi, Frank J., ed., *The Handbook of Fixed Income Securities*, 2d ed. (Homewood, Illinois: Dow Jones-Irwin, 1987).

McMillan, Lawrence G., *Options as a Strategic Investment*, 2d ed. (New York: New York Institute of Finance, 1986).

Oberhofer, George D., *Rate Risk Management: Fixed Income Strategies Using Futures, Options and Swaps* (Chicago: Probus Publishing Company, 1988).

Siegel, Daniel R., and Diane F. Siegel, *The Futures Markets: Arbitrage, Risk Management and Portfolio Strategies* (Chicago: Probus Publishing Company, 1990).

Smith, Jr., Clifford W., Charles W. Smithson, and D. Sykes Wilford, *Managing Financial Risk* (New York: HarperCollins, 1990).

Financial Accounting Standards Board Statement No. 80, Futures Contracts.

OCC Documents

Bank Accounting Advisory Series, Issue No. 1, June 1990.

Comptroller's Handbook for National Bank Examiners, Section 203 (Washington, D.C., March 1990).

Banking Circular 79 (3rd Rev.), National Bank Participation in the Financial Futures and Forward Placement Markets, April 19, 1983.

Forwards

I. Product Description

A forward contract is a customized obligation to receive or deliver a specified amount of a commodity or security, at a specified price, at a specific date in the future. The terms of the contract are negotiated directly by the counterparties and can only be terminated with the consent of both parties. The contract is sold or bought immediately, but not paid for until some future date. This feature, along with the lack of an exchange acting as an intermediary, gives forwards credit risk not evident in futures contracts.

Forward contracts are the oldest and simplest of the off-balance sheet products. They are very similar to a futures contract except there is no organized exchange present, no daily settlement, and no margin requirement. Since forwards are not standardized instruments, they can be negotiated on virtually any commodity or financial instrument. However, the most common forwards used by commercial banks are interest rate forwards and foreign exchange forwards. Commodity forward contracts may become more important to commercial banks with the increased activity in the commodity markets.

A foreign exchange forward contract is a contract to deliver or receive a specified amount of a foreign currency, at a specified price, at some date in the future. These contracts allow banks to hedge foreign currency risk by locking in a rate now, for delivery later. The advantage of a foreign exchange forward over a future is that it can be customized to the particular needs of the customer. For example, if a bank has foreign currency exposure that is longer than the available futures contract in that currency, it could enter into a forward contract at the required date and avoid the risk of rolling over the futures position when the longest contract expires.

Interest rate forwards, or forward rate agreements (FRAs), are contracts to pay or receive a specified interest rate, at a specified date in the future, on a specified notional amount. FRAs are agreements on interest rates only, not to make loans or receive deposits.

II. Market—Where to Find Current Value and Ratings

Forward contracts are not traded on organized exchanges, thus there is no readily available published market value. Dealers of forward contracts will quote prices based on the terms of the contracts, but no published price quotes are available.

III. What You Should Look for (Suitability)

Forward contracts are legitimate risk management products that banks may use to hedge exposure to interest rate and currency price movements. The most important hedging feature is that the contracts are negotiated between the parties and not established by an exchange. This adds flexibility and allows a bank to hedge risks that go beyond the maturity of available futures or options contracts. For example, a bank has a loan to fund in three years because of a commitment issued by the loan department. It desires to hedge against rates rising above the agreed upon funding price. Because futures contracts do not extend three years, the bank could instead enter into a forward rate agreement in which it will receive the loan price less a spread, three years into the future. This way the bank will not be exposed to rates rising and being unable to fund the loan at a profitable rate. Forwards can be used when a bank has interest rate or foreign currency exposure that exists beyond the available futures strip or has other unique circumstances.

Speculating using forward contracts should only be done by banks with strong capital and the management sophistication required to manage risks of this type.

The examiner must ensure that bank management understands the risks associated with these products and implements systems and controls to effectively quantify and manage those risks. Specifically, this will include an analysis of the following:

Policies: Management must implement specific written policies that authorize the activities in which the bank will engage. The policies should set limits for all the various risks associated with these products including, but not limited to, position limits, maturity limits, credit limits, and earnings-at-risk limits that should be incorporated into the risk management system used by the bank.

Procedures: Management must establish procedures and internal controls to ensure that policy limits are enforced. Procedures should be written for credit approval; segregation of duties in operations; revaluation, if necessary; and, provision of periodic reports to management.

Risk Management System: The risk management system must include a model to quantify accurately the risk associated with the position and provide the means to effectively manage that risk. The risk should be monitored relative to the limits imposed by the policies. In hedging situations, correlation studies for the appropriate instruments should detail the mechanics of the hedge. Examiners must ensure the accuracy of the models used to measure and monitor the risk. This may include modeling earnings of the position or the gains and losses associated with given hedges and comparing them to the expected result. The system must incorporate all risks associated with the product and reflect them accurately relative to limits on earnings at risk.

Audit: Internal and external audits should be performed. Examiners must determine the adequacy of each. This should particularly focus on the effectiveness of internal controls and the adequacy of the management information system. This area should also address management's willingness to implement the proper control systems to monitor activities of this sophistication. Examiners will also determine the expertise of the auditors.

The lack of the above information may lead to unsafe and unsound banking practices.

IV. Accounting Treatment

A bank engaging in forwards should have accounting policies and procedures that include recordkeeping requirements and methods for determining whether forwards are reducing risk or increasing risk and for accounting for each forward contract, based on its type and purpose. Accounting policies and procedures for forwards should be approved by the board of directors. They should be designed to ensure consistent and appropriate accounting for forward contracts.

Accounting for forwards should follow the requirements of the Call Report Instructions. The Call Report requires banks to account for forwards consistently, either at market value or at the lower of cost or market value.

Market values on all forwards should be determined at least monthly, or more often, if the bank has a material amount of these contracts.

The par value of outstanding forwards should be reported in Call Report Schedule RC-L "Off-Balance Sheet Items." For reporting purposes, contracts are considered outstanding until they have been cancelled by acquisition or delivery of the underlying security.

For forwards accounted for on a mark-to-market basis, net valuation gains should be reported as other noninterest income in the Call Report. Net valuation losses should be reported as other noninterest expense. For forwards accounted for on a lower of cost or market basis, write-downs to market are recorded as other noninterest expense on the Call Report.

Note that regulatory accounting does not permit loss or gain deferral for forwards (hedge accounting). In other words, a bank accounts for these contracts the same, whether they are entered into for speculative or hedging purposes. The only exception to this policy is for mortgage banking operations. Banks are permitted to use hedge accounting for mortgage banking operations.

V. Risks

Interest Rate Risk: Varies with the type and use of the contract. Forward contracts should be used to reduce interest rate exposure rather than speculate on future interest rate movements.

Credit Risk: Substantial since no cash is exchanged until the maturity of the contract. Management must effectively measure and manage this risk by incorporating proper credit procedures to analyze the credit risk with each counterparty with whom it participates.

Liquidity Risk: Limited, since the forward currency and interest rate markets are sophisticated, liquid markets. However, liquidity will vary among different contracts and management must understand and monitor liquidity risk in the forward portfolio.

Other Risk: Settlement Risk: Settlement risk will exist at the time the contract calls for delivery. Settlement limits should be established to limit this risk to the extent possible.

VI. Legal Limitations

Forwards are not considered investment securities under 12 U.S.C. 24(7). However, the use of these contracts is considered to be an activity incidental to banking, within safe and sound banking principles. Refer to subsection III, Suitability, in this section for details on systems, controls, and limits that bank management must implement prior to engaging in forward contract activities.

VII. Risk-based Capital Requirement

Foreign exchange, commodity and interest rate contracts have the following process for determining the risk-based capital requirement. The three steps determine: the current credit exposure; the potential credit exposure; and, the risk-weight. Additional details follow:

1. Mark to market (positive values only).

2. Add-on for potential credit exposure:

   — Interest Rate 0 % ($\leq$ 1 Yr.) .5 % (> 1 Yr.)
   — Exchange Rate 1 % ($\leq$ 1 Yr.) 5 % (> 1 Yr.)

3. Assign to Risk Category, Maximum 50 percent.

The risk-based capital requirement is computed by multiplying the sum of the current and potential credit exposure (step one plus step two) *by* the risk weight (step three).

Note also that exchange rate contracts that have an original maturity of 14 calendar days or less and instruments traded on exchanges and subject to daily margin requirements are exempt from the risk-based capital calculation.

(Further details relative to risk-based capital calculation can be found in the *Comptroller's Manual for National Banks* under 12 CFR 3.1, Appendix A. If the regulation is still not clear, the Chief National Bank Examiner's Office can assist in finding an answer.)

VIII. References

Fabozzi, Frank J., ed., *The Handbook of Fixed Income Securities*, 2d ed. (Homewood, Illinois: Dow Jones-Irwin, 1987).

McMillan, Lawrence G., *Options as a Strategic Investment*, 2d ed. (New York: New York Institute of Finance, 1986).

Oberhofer, George D., *Rate Risk Management: Fixed Income Strategies Using Futures, Options and Swaps* (Chicago: Probus Publishing Company, 1988).

Siegel, Daniel R., and Diane F. Siegel, *The Futures Markets: Arbitrage, Risk Management and Portfolio Strategies* (Chicago: Probus Publishing Company, 1990).

Smith, Jr., Clifford W., Charles W. Smithson, and D. Sykes Wilford, *Managing Financial Risk* (New York: HarperCollins, 1990).

OCC Documents

Bank Accounting Advisory Series, Issue No. 1, June 1990.

Comptroller's Handbook for National Bank Examiners, Section 203 (Washington, D.C., March 1990).

Banking Circular 79 (3rd Rev.), National Bank Participation in the Financial Futures and Forward Placement Markets, April 19, 1983.

Appendix B: Excerpts from FASB Statement No. 115

Statement of Financial Accounting Standards No. 115

Accounting for Certain Investments in Debt and Equity Securities

May 1993

INTRODUCTION

1. This Statement addresses the accounting and reporting for certain investments in **debt securities**[1] and **equity securities.** It expands the use of **fair value** accounting for those securities but retains the use of the amortized cost method for investments in debt securities that the reporting enterprise has the positive intent and ability to hold to maturity.

2. This Statement was undertaken mainly in response to concerns expressed by regulators and others about the recognition and measurement of investments in debt securities, particularly those held by financial institutions. They questioned the appropriateness of using the amortized cost method for certain investments in debt securities in light of certain trading and sales practices. Their concerns also were prompted by the existence of inconsistent guidance on the reporting of debt securities held as assets in various AICPA Audit and Accounting Guides. The AICPA's Accounting Standards Executive Committee (AcSEC) and the major CPA firms, among others, urged the Board to reexamine the accounting for certain investments in **securities.**

STANDARDS OF FINANCIAL ACCOUNTING AND REPORTING

Scope

3. Except as indicated in paragraph 4, this Statement establishes standards of financial accounting and reporting for investments in equity securities that have readily determinable fair values and for all investments in debt securities.

a. The fair value of an equity security is readily determinable if sales prices or bid-and-asked quotations are currently available on a securities exchange registered

---

[1] Words that appear in the glossary in Appendix C are set in **boldface type** the first time they appear.

with the Securities and Exchange Commission (SEC) or in the over-the-counter market, provided that those prices or quotations for the over-the-counter market are publicly reported by the National Association of Securities Dealers Automated Quotations systems or by the National Quotation Bureau. Restricted stock[2] does not meet that definition.

b. The fair value of an equity security traded only in a foreign market is readily determinable if that foreign market is of a breadth and scope comparable to one of the U.S. markets referred to above.

c. The fair value of an investment in a mutual fund is readily determinable if the fair value per share (unit) is determined and published and is the basis for current transactions.

4. This Statement does not apply to investments in equity securities accounted for under the equity method nor to investments in consolidated subsidiaries. This Statement does not apply to enterprises whose specialized accounting practices include accounting for substantially all investments in debt and equity securities at market value or fair value, with changes in value recognized in earnings (income) or in the change in net assets. Examples of those enterprises are brokers and dealers in securities, defined benefit pension plans, and investment companies. This Statement also does not apply to not-for-profit organizations; however, it does apply to cooperatives and mutual enterprises, including credit unions and mutual insurance companies.

5. This Statement supersedes FASB Statement No. 12, *Accounting for Certain Marketable Securities,* and supersedes or amends other accounting pronouncements listed in Appendix B.

Accounting for Certain Investments in Debt and Equity Securities

6. At acquisition, an enterprise shall classify debt and equity securities into one of three categories: held-to-maturity, available-for-sale, or trading. At each reporting date, the appropriateness of the classification shall be reassessed.

---

[2]*Restricted stock,* for the purpose of this Statement, means equity securities for which sale is restricted by governmental or contractual requirement (other than in connection with being pledged as collateral) except if that requirement terminates within one year or if the holder has the power by contract or otherwise to cause the requirement to be met within one year. Any portion of the security that can be reasonably expected to qualify for sale within one year, such as may be the case under Rule 144 or similar rules of the SEC, is not considered restricted.

2

Held-to-Maturity Securities

7. Investments in debt securities shall be classified as *held-to-maturity* and measured at amortized cost in the statement of financial position only if the reporting enterprise has the positive intent and ability to hold those securities to maturity.

8. The following changes in circumstances, however, may cause the enterprise to change its intent to hold a certain security to maturity without calling into question its intent to hold other debt securities to maturity in the future. Thus, the sale or transfer of a held-to-maturity security due to one of the following changes in circumstances shall not be considered to be inconsistent with its original classification:

a. Evidence of a significant deterioration in the issuer's creditworthiness
b. A change in tax law that eliminates or reduces the tax-exempt status of interest on the debt security (but not a change in tax law that revises the marginal tax rates applicable to interest income)
c. A major business combination or major disposition (such as sale of a segment) that necessitates the sale or transfer of held-to-maturity securities to maintain the enterprise's existing interest rate risk position or credit risk policy
d. A change in statutory or regulatory requirements significantly modifying either what constitutes a permissible investment or the maximum level of investments in certain kinds of securities, thereby causing an enterprise to dispose of a held-to-maturity security
e. A significant increase by the regulator in the industry's capital requirements that causes the enterprise to downsize by selling held-to-maturity securities
f. A significant increase in the risk weights of debt securities used for regulatory risk-based capital purposes.

In addition to the foregoing changes in circumstances, other events that are isolated, nonrecurring, and unusual for the reporting enterprise that could not have been reasonably anticipated may cause the enterprise to sell or transfer a held-to-maturity security without necessarily calling into question its intent to hold other debt securities to maturity. All sales and transfers of held-to-maturity securities shall be disclosed pursuant to paragraph 22.

9. An enterprise shall not classify a debt security as held-to-maturity if the enterprise has the intent to hold the security for only an indefinite period. Consequently,

a debt security should not, for example, be classified as held-to-maturity if the enterprise anticipates that the security would be available to be sold in response to:

a. Changes in market interest rates and related changes in the security's prepayment risk
b. Needs for liquidity (for example, due to the withdrawal of deposits, increased demand for loans, surrender of insurance policies, or payment of insurance claims)
c. Changes in the availability of and the yield on alternative investments
d. Changes in funding sources and terms
e. Changes in foreign currency risk.

10. Although its asset-liability management may encompass consideration of the maturity and repricing characteristics of all investments in debt securities, an enterprise may decide that it can accomplish the necessary adjustments under its asset-liability management without having all of its debt securities available for disposition. In that case, the enterprise may choose to designate certain debt securities as unavailable to be sold to accomplish those ongoing adjustments deemed necessary under its asset-liability management, thereby enabling those debt securities to be accounted for at amortized cost on the basis of a positive intent and ability to hold them to maturity.

11. Sales of debt securities that meet either of the following two conditions may be considered as maturities for purposes of the classification of securities under paragraphs 7 and 12 and the disclosure requirements under paragraph 22:

a. The sale of a security occurs near enough to its maturity date (or call date if exercise of the call is probable) that interest rate risk is substantially eliminated as a pricing factor. That is, the date of sale is so near the maturity or call date (for example, within three months) that changes in market interest rates would not have a significant effect on the security's fair value.
b. The sale of a security occurs after the enterprise has already collected a substantial portion (at least 85 percent) of the principal outstanding at acquisition due either to prepayments on the debt security or to scheduled payments on a debt security payable in equal installments (both principal and interest) over its term. For variable-rate securities, the scheduled payments need not be equal.

4

Trading Securities and Available-for-Sale Securities

12. Investments in debt securities that are not classified as held-to-maturity and equity securities that have readily determinable fair values shall be classified in one of the following categories and measured at fair value in the statement of financial position:

a. *Trading securities.* Securities that are bought and held principally for the purpose of selling them in the near term (thus held for only a short period of time) shall be classified as *trading securities.* Trading generally reflects active and frequent buying and selling, and trading securities are generally used with the objective of generating profits on short-term differences in price. Mortgage-backed securities that are held for sale in conjunction with mortgage banking activities, as described in FASB Statement No. 65, *Accounting for Certain Mortgage Banking Activities,* shall be classified as trading securities. (Other mortgage-backed securities not held for sale in conjunction with mortgage banking activities shall be classified based on the criteria in this paragraph and paragraph 7.)

b. *Available-for-sale securities.* Investments not classified as trading securities (nor as held-to-maturity securities) shall be classified as *available-for-sale securities.*

Reporting Changes in Fair Value

13. Unrealized **holding gains and losses** for trading securities shall be included in earnings. Unrealized holding gains and losses for available-for-sale securities (including those classified as current assets) shall be excluded from earnings and reported as a net amount in a separate component of shareholders' equity until realized. Paragraph 36 of FASB Statement No. 109, *Accounting for Income Taxes,* provides guidance on reporting the tax effects of unrealized holding gains and losses reported in a separate component of shareholders' equity.

14. Dividend and interest income, including amortization of the premium and discount arising at acquisition, for all three categories of investments in securities shall continue to be included in earnings. This Statement does not affect the methods used for recognizing and measuring the amount of dividend and interest income. Realized gains and losses for securities classified as either available-for-sale or held-to-maturity also shall continue to be reported in earnings.

Transfers between Categories of Investments

15. The transfer of a security between categories of investments shall be accounted for at fair value.[3] At the date of the transfer, the security's unrealized holding gain or loss shall be accounted for as follows:

a. For a security transferred from the trading category, the unrealized holding gain or loss at the date of the transfer will have already been recognized in earnings and shall not be reversed.
b. For a security transferred into the trading category, the unrealized holding gain or loss at the date of the transfer shall be recognized in earnings immediately.
c. For a debt security transferred into the available-for-sale category from the held-to-maturity category, the unrealized holding gain or loss at the date of the transfer shall be recognized in a separate component of shareholders' equity.
d. For a debt security transferred into the held-to-maturity category from the available-for-sale category, the unrealized holding gain or loss at the date of the transfer shall continue to be reported in a separate component of shareholders' equity but shall be amortized over the remaining life of the security as an adjustment of yield in a manner consistent with the amortization of any premium or discount. The amortization of an unrealized holding gain or loss reported in equity will offset or mitigate the effect on interest income of the amortization of the premium or discount (discussed in footnote 3) for that held-to-maturity security.

Consistent with paragraphs 7-9, transfers from the held-to-maturity category should be rare, except for transfers due to the changes in circumstances identified in subparagraphs 8(a)-8(f). Given the nature of a trading security, transfers into or from the trading category also should be rare.

Impairment of Securities

16. For individual securities classified as either available-for-sale or held-to-maturity, an enterprise shall determine whether a decline in fair value below the amortized cost basis is other than temporary. For example, if it is probable that the investor will be unable to collect all amounts due according to the contractual terms of a debt security not impaired at acquisition, an other-than-temporary im-

---

[3] For a debt security transferred into the held-to-maturity category, the use of fair value may create a premium or discount that, under amortized cost accounting, shall be amortized thereafter as an adjustment of yield pursuant to FASB Statement No. 91, *Accounting for Nonrefundable Fees and Costs Associated with Originating or Acquiring Loans and Initial Direct Costs of Leases.*

pairment shall be considered to have occurred.[4] If the decline in fair value is judged to be other than temporary, the cost basis of the individual security shall be written down to fair value as a new cost basis and the amount of the write-down shall be included in earnings (that is, accounted for as a realized loss). The new cost basis shall not be changed for subsequent recoveries in fair value. Subsequent increases in the fair value of available-for-sale securities shall be included in the separate component of equity pursuant to paragraph 13; subsequent decreases in fair value, if not an other-than-temporary impairment, also shall be included in the separate component of equity.

Financial Statement Presentation

17. An enterprise that presents a classified statement of financial position shall report all trading securities as current assets and shall report individual held-to-maturity securities and individual available-for-sale securities as either current or noncurrent, as appropriate, under the provisions of ARB No. 43, Chapter 3A, "Working Capital—Current Assets and Current Liabilities."[5]

18. Cash flows from purchases, sales, and maturities of available-for-sale securities and held-to-maturity securities shall be classified as cash flows from investing activities and reported gross for each security classification in the statement of cash flows. Cash flows from purchases, sales, and maturities of trading securities shall be classified as cash flows from operating activities.

---

[4] A decline in the value of a security that is other than temporary is also discussed in AICPA Auditing Interpretation, *Evidential Matter for the Carrying Amount of Marketable Securities,* which was issued in 1975 and incorporated in Statement on Auditing Standards No. 1, *Codification of Auditing Standards and Procedures,* as Interpretation 20, and in SEC Staff Accounting Bulletin No. 59, *Accounting for Noncurrent Marketable Equity Securities.*

[5] Chapter 3A of ARB 43 indicates in paragraph 4 that "the term *current assets* is used to designate cash and other assets or resources commonly identified as those which are reasonably expected to be realized in cash or sold or consumed during the normal operating cycle of the business." That paragraph further indicates that the term also comprehends "marketable securities representing the investment of cash available for current operations." Paragraph 5 indicates that "a one-year time period is to be used as a basis for the segregation of current assets in cases where there are several operating cycles occurring within a year."

Disclosures

19. For securities classified as available-for-sale and separately for securities classified as held-to-maturity, all reporting enterprises shall disclose the aggregate fair value, gross unrealized holding gains, gross unrealized holding losses, and amortized cost basis by major security type as of each date for which a statement of financial position is presented. In complying with this requirement, financial institutions[6] shall include in their disclosure the following major security types, though additional types also may be included as appropriate:

a. Equity securities
b. Debt securities issued by the U.S. Treasury and other U.S. government corporations and agencies
c. Debt securities issued by states of the United States and political subdivisions of the states
d. Debt securities issued by foreign governments
e. Corporate debt securities
f. Mortgage-backed securities
g. Other debt securities.

20. For investments in debt securities classified as available-for-sale and separately for securities classified as held-to-maturity, all reporting enterprises shall disclose information about the contractual maturities of those securities as of the date of the most recent statement of financial position presented. Maturity information may be combined in appropriate groupings. In complying with this requirement, financial institutions shall disclose the fair value and the amortized cost of debt securities based on at least 4 maturity groupings: (a) within 1 year, (b) after 1 year through 5 years, (c) after 5 years through 10 years, and (d) after 10 years. Securities not due at a single maturity date, such as mortgage-backed securities, may be disclosed separately rather than allocated over several maturity groupings; if allocated, the basis for allocation also shall be disclosed.

---

[6]For purposes of the disclosure requirements of paragraphs 19 and 20, the term *financial institutions* includes banks, savings and loan associations, savings banks, credit unions, finance companies, and insurance companies, consistent with the usage of that term in AICPA Statement of Position 90-11, *Disclosure of Certain Information by Financial Institutions About Debt Securities Held as Assets*.

21. For each period for which the results of operations are presented, an enterprise shall disclose:

a. The proceeds from sales of available-for-sale securities and the gross realized gains and gross realized losses on those sales
b. The basis on which cost was determined in computing realized gain or loss (that is, specific identification, average cost, or other method used)
c. The gross gains and gross losses included in earnings from transfers of securities from the available-for-sale category into the trading category
d. The change in net unrealized holding gain or loss on available-for-sale securities that has been included in the separate component of shareholders' equity during the period
e. The change in net unrealized holding gain or loss on trading securities that has been included in earnings during the period.

22. For any sales of or transfers from securities classified as held-to-maturity, the amortized cost amount of the sold or transferred security, the related realized or unrealized gain or loss, and the circumstances leading to the decision to sell or transfer the security shall be disclosed in the notes to the financial statements for each period for which the results of operations are presented. Such sales or transfers should be rare, except for sales and transfers due to the changes in circumstances identified in subparagraphs 8(a)-8(f).

Effective Date and Transition

23. This Statement shall be effective for fiscal years beginning after December 15, 1993. Except as indicated in the following paragraph, initial application of this Statement shall be as of the beginning of an enterprise's fiscal year; at that date, investments in debt and equity securities owned shall be classified based on the enterprise's current intent. Earlier application as of the beginning of a fiscal year is permitted only in financial statements for fiscal years beginning after issuance of this Statement. This Statement may not be applied retroactively to prior years' financial statements.

24. For fiscal years beginning prior to December 16, 1993, enterprises are permitted to initially apply this Statement as of the end of a fiscal year for which annual financial statements have not previously been issued. This Statement may not be applied retroactively to the interim financial statements for that year.

25. The effect on retained earnings of initially applying this Statement shall be reported as the effect of a change in accounting principle in a manner similar to the cumulative effect of a change in accounting principle as described in paragraph 20

of APB Opinion No. 20, *Accounting Changes*. That effect on retained earnings includes the reversal of amounts previously included in earnings that would be excluded from earnings under this Statement (refer to paragraph 13). The unrealized holding gain or loss, net of tax effect, for securities classified as available-for-sale as of the date that this Statement is first applied shall be an adjustment of the balance of the separate component of equity. The pro forma effects of retroactive application (discussed in paragraph 21 of Opinion 20) shall not be disclosed.

> **The provisions of this Statement need
> not be applied to immaterial items.**

This Statement was adopted by the affirmative votes of five members of the Financial Accounting Standards Board. Messrs. Sampson and Swieringa dissented.

Messrs. Sampson and Swieringa disagree with the accounting treatment prescribed in paragraphs 6-18 of this Statement because it does not resolve two of the most important problems that caused the Board to address the accounting for certain investments in debt and equity securities—namely, accounting based on intent, and gains trading. They believe that those problems can only be resolved by reporting all securities that are within the scope of this Statement at fair value and by including unrealized changes in fair value in earnings.

This Statement requires that debt securities be classified as held-to-maturity, available-for-sale, or trading and that securities in each classification be accounted for differently. As a result, three otherwise identical debt securities could receive three different accounting treatments within the same enterprise. Moreover, classification of debt securities as held-to-maturity is based on management's positive intent and ability to hold to maturity. The notion of intent to hold to maturity (a) is subjective at best, (b) is not likely to be consistently applied, (c) given the provisions in paragraphs 8-11, is not likely to be descriptive of actual transactions and events, and (d) disregards the best available information about the present value of expected future cash flows from a readily marketable debt security—namely, its observable market price. Effective management of financial activities increasingly requires a flexible approach to asset and liability management that is inconsistent with a hold-to-maturity notion.

This Statement also requires that certain debt securities classified as held-to-maturity be reported at amortized cost and that certain debt and equity securities classified as available-for-sale be reported at fair value with unrealized changes in fair value excluded from earnings. Those requirements provide the opportunity for the managers of an enterprise to manage its earnings by selectively selling securities

10

and thereby selectively including realized gains in earnings and selectively excluding unrealized losses from earnings. An impressive amount of empirical evidence indicates that many financial institutions have engaged in that behavior. That behavior undermines the relevance and reliability of accounting information.

The Board concluded that unrealized changes in fair value for trading securities should be reported in earnings because that reporting reflects the economic consequences of the events of the enterprise (such as changes in fair values) as well as the transactions (such as sales of securities) when those events and transactions occur and results in more relevant reporting (paragraph 92). However, the Board concluded that similar reporting of unrealized changes in fair value for available-for-sale securities has the potential for significant earnings volatility that is unrepresentative of both the way enterprises manage their businesses and the impact of economic events on the overall enterprise and, therefore, decided that those changes should be excluded from earnings (paragraphs 93 and 94). Those conclusions do not alleviate the potential for volatility in reported earnings; rather, they provide the opportunity for selective volatility in reported earnings—that is, the volatility in reported earnings that results from the recognition of unrealized changes in fair value in earnings through selective sales of securities.

Reporting all securities that are within the scope of this Statement at fair value and including unrealized changes in fair value in earnings would result in reflecting the consequences of economic events (price changes) in the periods in which they occur rather than when managers wish to selectively recognize those consequences in earnings. Messrs. Sampson and Swieringa believe that this reporting is the only way to resolve the problems of accounting based on intent and gains trading that have raised concerns about the relevance and credibility of accounting for certain investments in debt and equity securities.

In addition, Mr. Sampson is concerned that the conclusions adopted in this Statement may, in some cases, portray unrepresentative volatility in capital because enterprises are not permitted to recognize the unrealized changes in fair value of the liabilities that are related to investments accounted for as available-for-sale securities.

Members of the Financial Accounting Standards Board:

> Dennis R. Beresford, *Chairman*
> Joseph V. Anania
> Victor H. Brown
> James J. Leisenring
> Robert H. Northcutt
> A. Clarence Sampson
> Robert J. Swieringa

About the Author

John Bowen is a vice president and portfolio advisor with Wachovia Bank of Georgia's Bond and Money Market Group in Atlanta, where his clientele includes bankers from across the country. Through Wachovia, he is developing and presenting a series of seminars on FASB #115 and portfolio management.

Prior to Wachovia, Mr. Bowen worked for the international accounting firm Ernst & Young. He has had articles published in *Bank Accounting and Finance*, *Knight-Ridder Financial News* and the *ABA Banking Journal* and has taught investment courses at *The School for Bank Administration* and *The Banking School of the South*. Bowen's last book was *Investing in Mortgage Securities* (Bankers Publishing Company, 1989).